The Power
of the
Anointing

David Chapman

The Power of the Anointing

David Chapman

All Bible quotations are from the New King James Version unless otherwise noted.

TRU Publishing
P.O. Box 201
Thatcher, Arizona 85552

Table of Contents

The Anointing

One of the best ways to dig deep into a subject is to do word studies. It's important to understand the English word being used, but also the original language. The Old Testament was written mostly in Hebrew with some Aramaic (parts of Ezra and Daniel), while the New Testament was written in Greek.

It is also useful to look at how many times a word is used in the Bible. There are other considerations: how is the word used in the Old Testament compared to the New Testament? How is the word used the first time it is introduced? Context cannot be overlooked either. It has been said that, "A text without context is just a pretext."

For the above reasons, we will begin our study on the subject of the anointing by looking at the various words translated as "anoint" or "anointing" throughout the Bible.

Word Study
The word "anoint" or "anointing" is in the Bible 162 times in the King James Version.

- Anoint 35 times
- Anointed 98 times
- Anointest 1 times
- Anointing 28 times

There are several original Greek word translated "anoint" in the New Testament:

1. Chrio (khree-o), which means, "to smear with oil." It is the word Jesus used at the public announcement of His ministry (Luke 4:18).
2. Egchriō (en-khrē'-ō), which means, "to rub in," hence, "to besmear, to anoint" (Revelation 3:18).
3. Epichriō (e-pē-khrē'-ō), which means, "to spread on, anoint anything upon anything" (John 9:6).
4. Myrizō (mü-rē'-zō), which means, "to anoint the body for burial" (Mark 14:8).
5. Chrisma (khrē'-smä), which means, "anything smeared on, unguent, ointment, usually prepared by the Hebrews from oil and aromatic herbs." Used of the Holy Spirit (1 John 2:20, 27).
6. Aleipho (al-i-fo), which means, "To rub or smear (olive) oil on the body" (Mark 6:13).

In the Old Testament, there are also several different Hebrew words translated "anoint."

1. Balal (bä·lal'), which means, "to overflow, to mix" (Psalm 92:10)
2. Dashen (dä·shän'), which means, "To make fat, prosperous" (Psalm 23:5).
3. Yitshar (yits·här'), which means, "Fresh oil, shining (pure) oil" (Zechariah 4:14).
4. Mimshach (mim·shakh'), which means, "to anoint, expand" (Ezekiel 28:14 for Lucifer before he fell).

5. Mashach (maw-shakh), which means, "To rub with oil, to consecrate" (1 Samuel 16:13)
6. Mishchah (mēsh·khä'), which means, "consecrated portion, anointing oil, portion, ointment, anointing portion" (Exodus 40:15).
7. Mashiyach (mä·shē'·akh), which means, "Anointed One, Messiah" (Daniel 9:26).
8. Cuwk (sük), which means, "to pour in anointing" (Daniel 10:3).

The above information is to allow the student to study this topic of the anointing to the fullest. The Bible has much to say about this wonderful topic. Our focus will not be on the physical aspects of the anointing, as defined in some of the words, but on the spiritual side of the anointing.

Physical World vs. Spiritual World
There is a physical world and a spiritual world. The physical world is *seen* and the spiritual world is *unseen*. The blessing of God comes out of the spiritual world. If we, as Christians, are going to impact this world that we live in, we must learn how to bring the *dunamis* power of God out of the unseen world. God is looking for vessels to flow this power through. His power is the anointing of the Holy Spirit. He is not looking for perfect people. We are human and have flaws, but if we keep surrendering to God, He will pout through us.

2 Corinthians 4:7 But we have this treasure in earthen vessels, that the excellence of the power may be of God and not of us.

As believers, we must learn to walk by faith. Faith is the connecting force that draws the anointing from the unseen. When we were carnal unbelievers, we lived solely off of the intellect and the five senses that God gave us to connect with this physical world. Now that we are born again, divinely connected to the Lord Himself, we must train ourselves to no longer exist from the intellect and five senses. In fact, these attributes can become enemies of the anointing if they continue to rule.

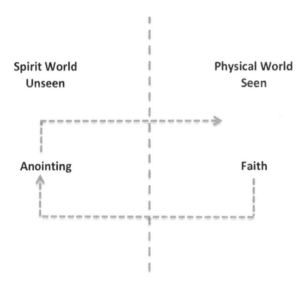

Spirit World
Unseen

Physical World
Seen

Anointing

Faith

The electrical power in your home has traveled a long distance to get to you. It is transformed to High Voltage in order to travel the distance needed, but must be transformed down before it is usable in your home. It can't just be blasted in. This is the way God's anointing works. God can't just dump all of His power on us. He is omnipotent – all-powerful. Faith is like the transformer to deliver the power and the anointing. It must be remembered that the transformer doesn't create the power; it just delivers the power. Faith takes the high voltage power of God and delivers it into the areas that are needed in a way that can be received and utilized.

What is the Anointing?

So, what is "the anointing?" To start with, it is something that we learn as a Spirit-filled Christian. As one little old lady said, "I may not know what the anointing is, but I know what it ain't." This, in fact, may be the best definition that you will find. It's so important to know when the anointing is NOT present – when the work being done is in the flesh. The flesh profits nothing, but the Spirit gives life.

> **John 6:63 It is the Spirit who gives life; the flesh profits nothing.**

If every church attender around the world experienced a sudden awareness of whether the anointing was present or absent, how many would leave if the answer were absent? As we will see when we examine the ministry of Jesus upon the earth, not everyone in church wants the presence of the anointing of the Holy Spirit.

There is both an anointing *within* us and also an anointing that comes *upon* us.

The Anointing Upon	The Anointing Within
The anointing is the ability of the Holy Spirit coming upon a human vessel in order to accomplish God's purpose. This purpose could not be accomplished by the works of	There is also an anointing within – the indwelling presence of the Holy Spirit. He teaches us all things that we need to know (1 John 2:20, 27).

the flesh and intellect, but only with God's power. The anointing that comes upon us is not permanent, but as needed.	The anointing within never leaves us.

Jesus did all of His miracles by the anointing of the Holy Spirit (Luke 4:18, Acts 10:38). The apostles did all of their works by the anointing as well (Luke 24:49, Acts 1:8).

God uses ordinary folks to do miraculous things. The apostles who Jesus chose were simple and ordinary men. They did not "glow in the dark." When ordinary believers step out in faith and obey the Holy Spirit, extraordinary things happen.

The River
My home church, The River, is a church where the anointing of God flows. Some may ask where the name "The River" came from. There are a few different verses that mention a river. One of them says that God will make a river in the desert (Isaiah 43:19). There are also a couple of verses related to the river that provide additional meaning to how the anointing works.

> **Psalm 46:4-5**
> **4 There is a river whose streams shall make glad the city of God, The holy place of the tabernacle of the Most High.**
> **5 God is in the midst of her, she shall not be moved**

The verses in Psalm 46 show us that there is a river in the city of God, but it's the streams from it that bring gladness and joy.

This speaks to the need of releasing the river of God that is in us when we come together to worship God. The streams are our expressions of praise and worship to God. When we come together, if we all sit on the presence of God and refuse to enter in, there will be no manifest presence of God in our midst.

It isn't the worship team's job to get us to worship; their focus should be entirely upon the Lord and ministering to Him. As we join in, God becomes enthroned upon our praises and He inhabits them (Psalm 22:3).

> **John 7:38-39**
> **38 He who believes in Me, as the Scripture has said, out of his heart will flow rivers of living water."**
> **39 But this He spoke concerning the Spirit, whom those believing in Him would receive; for the Holy Spirit was not yet given, because Jesus was not yet glorified.**

Here, Jesus tells us that the river is the flow of the Holy Spirit within us. At that time, He had not been given into the earth. When Jesus ascended to the Father, the Holy Spirit descended. Now, as New Testament believers, the Holy Spirit lives in us – we are His temple.

> **1 Corinthians 3:16 Do you not know that you are the temple of God and that the Spirit of God dwells in you?**

Let's look at some aspects of a natural river:

- Rivers start at a high point, like a mountain
- Rivers form by merging with other streams

- Rivers don't just flow, but also change the surface of the earth
- Rivers, over time, cut rocks, move boulders, carve away all that is in its path

Spiritual rivers – the anointing – is much the same way. They begin at a high point with God and form as like-minded believers gather together as one. Like a river changes the surface of the earth over time, people are changed by sitting under the anointing and partaking of God's presence. Big problems become small problems under the force of the river of God's anointing.

Quenching & Grieving the Spirit

God no longer dwells in buildings made with human hands. He lives and dwells in us. Believers should be "God-inside-minded." There is a river inside of each one of us. But we can choose to dam up the river and not allow the Holy Spirit to manifest. The Bible clearly tells us that the Holy Spirit may be quenched and He may be grieved.

1 Thessalonians 5: 19 Do not quench the Spirit.

Ephesians 4:30 And do not grieve the Holy Spirit of God, by whom you were sealed for the day of redemption.

When the Holy Spirit is quenched, His hands are tied. As Psalm 78:41 says, we "limit the Holy One of Israel." The Greek word for "quench" (*sbennymi*) means, "to extinguish, to suppress." To suppress means to curtail, to prohibit or to deliberately exclude. When we come together and put limits on what God will do, we quench the anointing and power of the Holy Spirit. Some churches have programmed the Holy Spirit right out the door.

The Greek word for "grieve" (*lypeo*) means to "to offend, to make sorrowful, to make uneasy." The Holy Spirit is a Gentleman; He will not manifest where people are offending Him and making Him uneasy with their attitudes. "Religious" crowds tend to be very uptight. When we put "our program" above the leading of the Holy Spirit, we grieve Him. When we override what He wants done, we grieve Him. The Holy Spirit being grieved is His reaction to what we do to Him.

Quenching the Spirit	Grieving the Spirit
What we do to the Holy Spirit. Some examples:	How the Holy Spirit responds to what we have done to Him. Some examples:
<ul><li>Substitute our intellect for the wisdom of the Holy Spirit</li><li>Override His direction with our program</li><li>Worry about offending people with the Truth of God's Word</li><li>Operating in doubt and unbelief</li><li>Refusal to repent when the Spirit convicts</li></ul>	<ul><li>Removal of the anointing</li><li>No conviction of sin</li><li>Brass heavens</li><li>Absence of joy</li><li>No liberty</li></ul>

Traditional churches have been in steep decline for decades. Meanwhile, Spirit-filled churches have been exploding in growth during that same time period. The Pentecostal/ Charismatic movement has grown from just hundreds in the early 1900's to almost 600 million worldwide today.

Please don't misunderstand me to say that all Pentecostal/ Charismatic churches are flowing in the Spirit. That would be far from the truth. I am speaking mainly in generalities at this point. These churches have grown because of the way they began, with the free move of the Spirit, but they too can come under bondage to tradition and legalism.

Liberty

God wants the freedom and liberty of the Holy Spirit to flow in His house.

> **2 Corinthians 3:17 Now the Lord is the Spirit; and where the Spirit of the Lord is, there is liberty.**

Liberty will move people out and beyond their normal comfort zones. The religious crowd on the day of Pentecost thought that the disciples were drunk (Acts 2:13) because of the manifestation of the Spirit and the activities taking place. Some folks come into The River and realize that we are different than normal churches and leave. But God wants us to dive into The River and swim. He is calling us to let go of our inhibitions and fear of man – to worship the Lord in spirit and truth (John 4:24).

There are many people out there who are oppressed and defeated. We have no power outside of the Holy Spirit whereby to set them free. The anointing has power to destroy the works of the devil and set people free.

> **Isaiah 10:27 And the yoke shall be destroyed because of the anointing.**

Flow

Like a river, the Holy Spirit anointing will have a flow. Choppiness is an indication of the lack of anointing. When God's people get in the Spirit, there will be a beautiful symmetry to the events taking place. The prayer, the worship, the preaching, and the ministry will all flow together by the hand of God.

I'm reminded of the story in 2 Kings 3 where Elisha wasn't in the mood to prophesy when Jehoshaphat requested a word from the Lord. He had seen enough hypocrisy in the land and wasn't going to oblige. However, because he knew that Jehoshaphat was following the one true God, he agreed. However, Elisha didn't jump right in and begin to prophesy. He called for the minstrel to come and play. He understood the power of getting in a flow of the Spirit and that music was one of the tools that God used.

> **2 Kings 3:14-16**
> **14 And Elisha said, "*As* the Lord of hosts lives, before whom I stand, surely were it not that I regard the presence of Jehoshaphat king of Judah, I would not look at you, nor see you.**
> **15 But now bring me a musician." Then it happened, when the musician played, that the hand of the Lord came upon him.**
> **16 And he said, "Thus says the Lord…"**

The hand of the Lord came upon Elisha as the musician played and he began to prophesy. This flow happens in the church when we get in the Spirit.

Additionally, we must not be so quick to get out of the flow of the Spirit with sudden changes of direction during our meetings. It is best to linger before moving on or change directions. I've been in meetings where the anointing for worship was very strong and at a set time, someone would appear at the podium to read announcements. This kind of activity quenches the flow of the Holy Spirit. I'm not saying to not give announcements. I am saying be sensitive to the Spirit in all that you do and be cautious with sudden changes.

The meaning of the word "flow" is, "to exhibit smooth or graceful continuity, to move or progress freely, to be present in abundance." This is very descriptive of how the anointing works – it too is a flow in the Spirit.

Sometimes we "miss it" here and there. This happens for a number of reasons. Let's use a song as an example. The song may be awesome, with beautiful, scripturally based lyrics, but when performed, there's no divine connection with the congregation. In fact, it seems to break the anointing that was flowing up to that point. Should we just keep hammering away with the song until people "get it" or move on? In most cases, it is best to move on. As one preacher said, a song is like flying a kite. Sometimes, no matter how great the song, it doesn't fly.

On the other hand, if a song is flowing and people are responding with heart-felt worship, we shouldn't be so quick to move on to the next song. I always tell out worship leader that I don't care if we do the same song for 30 minutes as long as it's anointed.

When the anointing is flowing it is like what is described in Psalm 133.

> **133 Behold, how good and how pleasant it is**
> **For brethren to dwell together in unity!**
> **2 It is like the precious oil upon the head,**
> **Running down on the beard,**
> **The beard of Aaron,**
> **Running down on the edge of his garments.**
> **3 It is like the dew of Hermon,**
> **Descending upon the mountains of Zion;**
> **For there the Lord commanded the blessing—**
> **Life forevermore.**

The anointing that is upon the Head – Jesus – will flow down upon the body. In that place, the Lord will command His blessing.

The books Joel (2:23) in the Old Testament and James (5:7) in the New Testament speak of the times of the early rain and the latter rain. The early rain was fulfilled on the day of Pentecost and the days of the early church during the first century. The time of the latter rain began in the 20th century and will continue to the final hour.

Points for Reflection

- All of the Hebrew (OT) and Greek (NT) words for anoint or anointing are similar in meaning. To summarize, the word means, "To smear with oil, to overflow, to make fat"

- Faith is the connecting force that draws the anointing from the unseen.

- There is an anointing within that is permanent and there is an anointing upon that is only as needed.

- The Bible tells us that the Holy Spirit may be quenched and He may be grieved.

Anointing with Oil

There are several types or symbols of the Holy Spirit found in Scripture. Oil is one of these types.

- Rain (Joel 2:23-29)
- River (John 7:37-39)
- Wind (John 3:8)
- Wine (Ephesians 5:8)
- Fire (Acts 2:3)
- Dove (Matthew 3:16)
- Oil (James 5:14-15)

From the Old Testament through to the New, oil has been used as a symbol of the Holy Spirit. Whenever God set apart a prophet, priest or king, they were anointed with oil, symbolizing the need for the Holy Spirit's work in their lives.

However, in this section, I want to focus on anointing with oil for the purpose of healing.

When Jesus sent out the 12, two by two, He gave them authority to act in His name. The Word says that they preached repentance, cast out devils and anointed the sick with oil and healed them.

Mark 6:12-13

12 So they went out and preached that people should repent.

13 And they cast out many demons, and anointed with oil many who were sick, and healed them.

They first preached repentance. Repentance is the key. To repent means to change your mind, to do a 180 toward God, away from your sin. More repentance is needed in the church today. If there were more repentance, there would be more healings and miracles.

The original Greek word for "anointed" in verse 13 is *aleipho* (al-i-fo) and means, "to rub or smear (olive) oil on the body." The disciples basically went out with nothing but learned quickly that the anointing of God was more than enough. If God calls and anoints, He will provide whatever is needed. I learned a long time ago that if God calls, there is nothing that man can take away from it; and if He doesn't call, there is nothing that man can do to add to it.

The second reference to anointing with oil for the purpose of healing is found in the book of James.

James 5:14-15

14 Is anyone among you sick? Let him call for the elders of the church, and let them pray over him, anointing him with oil in the name of the Lord.

15 And the prayer of faith will save the sick, and the Lord will raise him up. And if he has committed sins, he will be forgiven.

Here, we have a little more information about the anointing process than we found in Mark. James writes that if there are any who are sick in the church, that the Lord will raise them up. What an awesome promise. That is one of the benefits of belonging to a local church that practices the truth of God's Word. James wrote, "Is there any sick **among you**?" It's important that we remain among our brothers and sisters in Christ.

Verse 14 tells us that the person who is sick should "call for the elders of the church." This is an act of faith on the part of the one who is sick. Sometimes a well-meaning Christian will drag their friend or family member forward for prayer. There is no act of faith on the part of the one who is sick.

One of my favorite stories in the Gospels is the woman with the issue of blood. For 12 years she suffered. She spent all that she had on doctors, but the condition only grew worse. Then one day, she heard about Jesus. She determined that if she could just touch the hem of His garment that she would be made whole. As the story reads in Mark chapter 5 (verses 24-34), she pressed through the crowd, refusing to be denied, and touched Jesus. Immediately she was made whole. Jesus knew that someone had touched Him beyond the physical – with faith. He asked, "Who touched Me?" The disciples couldn't understand because many were touching Him in the physical. Jesus told that woman, "Your faith has made you whole."

That woman did three things that are important to note:

1. She heard about a healing Jesus (Romans 10:17 says, "Faith comes from hearing").

2. She confessed that she would be made whole (Mark 11:23 says to speak what you believe).
3. She acted on her faith and refused to be denied (James 2:17 says that "Faith without works is dead").

Too many times, people take the passive route and they have not because they ask not (James 4:3). If you are sick, call for the elders of the church.

When anointing with oil, the "prayer of faith" must be prayed. Anointing with oil and praying, "God, if it be Thy will, heal this person" is NOT the prayer of faith. There are different types of prayer and the prayer of faith is one where the revealed promises of God's Word are stood upon in faith.

Different Types of Prayer
• The prayer consecration • The prayer of agreement • The prayer of faith • The prayer of intercession • The prayer of worship • The prayer of binding and loosing

Further, James writes that if the sick person has been caught up in sin, that God will forgive and restore. The original Greek actually states, "Currently in a state of being sinful." Some people feel that they have to clean their lives up before the ask God for help. God is the only One who can cleanse you. He is willing to heal your body and forgive your sin at the same time.

One of my favorite Psalms is 103:

Psalm 103:2-3
2 Bless the Lord, O my soul, and forget not all His benefits:
3 Who forgives all your iniquities, Who heals all your diseases.

God forgives all our iniquities and heals all our diseases! This is the power of the gospel. Jesus shed His blood for the wholeness of man.

I especially like where James goes next in this passage.

James 5:16 (KJV) Confess your faults one to another, and pray one for another, that ye may be healed. The effectual fervent prayer of a righteous man availeth much.

The environment where the anointing of God flows is one where people are transparent with their faults. A "religious" environment will always quench the move of the Spirit. It did in Jesus' day, just as it does in ours.

If we are not being real and being repentant, the application of oil to someone's forehead is little more than applying more religious cosmetics. For the Holy Spirit to move like we want Him to, we must let go and let God!

I always tell my church that the Holy Spirit is never limited because we have too many faults, but only because we are prideful and are unwilling to confess them and pray for one another. Whenever we confess a fault, we destroy the stronghold of pride. God resists the proud but gives grace to the humble (James 4:6).

Points for Reflection

- There are several types or symbols of the Holy Spirit found in Scripture.

- Too many times, people take the passive route and they have not because they ask not (James 4:3).

- It's important to remember that there are different types of prayer found in Scripture.

- The environment where the anointing of God flows is one where people are transparent with their faults.

The Ministry of Jesus

When Jesus came to the earth, He temporarily laid aside the attributes of His deity.

> **Philippians 2:5-7**
> **5 Let this mind be in you which was also in Christ Jesus,**
> **6 who, being in the form of God, did not consider it robbery to be equal with God,**
> **7 but made Himself of no reputation, taking the form of a bondservant, and coming in the likeness of men.**

The original Greek word for "no reputation" is kenos (ken-os), which means, "to empty." Jesus did not cease being God while on the earth, but voluntarily limited His divine attributes. He was 100% God and, at the same time, 100% man. This is the miracle of the incarnation. An example of this limitation is found in Mark 13:32 where Jesus said that the Son did not know time of His own second coming. This was in reference to His earthly mission. The statement no longer applies to His current status seated at the right hand of the Father.

There are three main areas that describe the attributes of God:

1. His Omnipresence (to be everywhere at the same time)
2. His Omnipotence (to be all powerful)
3. His Omniscience (to be all knowing)

Jesus voluntarily laid aside these abilities from the time that He was in Mary's womb until the day He rose from the dead.

Jesus performed His ministry as *a man anointed by the Holy Spirit*. Before the age of 30, Jesus did no miracles. His first miracle was recorded in John chapter two – turning the water into wine. If you read the story, you will discover a key to the anointing for miracles. Jesus' mother said to those present, "Whatever He says to you, do it" (John 2:5). Obedience to the voice of the Lord – even when it seems foolish, will unlock miracles.

At the age of 30, Jesus entered His public ministry by being baptized by John the Baptist. At that point, the Holy Spirit descended upon Him like a dove.

> **Matthew 3:16 When He had been baptized, Jesus came up immediately from the water; and behold, the heavens were opened to Him, and He saw the Spirit of God descending like a dove and alighting upon Him.**

It is interesting that a dove has nine main feathers in its right wing and nine main feathers in its left wing. There are nine gifts of the Spirit (1 Corinthians 12) and nine fruits of the Spirit (Galatians 5). Further, a dove has five main feathers in its tail. There are five ministry gifts (Ephesians 4). Our Lord walked in the fullness of the gifts of the Spirit, the fruit of the Spirit and the ministry gifts.

Upon being baptized with the Spirit and subsequently tested, Jesus entered His hometown to announce His ministry. He went into His home synagogue in Nazareth and began to read from the book of Isaiah (chapter 61).

> **Luke 4:18-19**
> **18 "The Spirit of the Lord is upon Me, because He has anointed Me to preach the gospel to the poor; He has sent Me to heal the brokenhearted, to proclaim liberty to the captives and recovery of sight to the blind, to set at liberty those who are oppressed;**
> **19 To proclaim the acceptable year of the Lord.**

Jesus told the people that He was the fulfillment of this prophecy (v. 21). Instead of rejoicing, the people were filled with wrath and tried to push him over a cliff (vv. 28-29). Everyone is not excited about the anointing. Religion wants to stifle the anointing because it takes the control and the glory away from man.

There was a five-fold purpose for the anointing of the Holy Spirit upon Jesus.

a. Healing for the brokenhearted
b. Liberty to the captives
c. Recovery of sight to the blind
d. Liberty to the oppressed
e. Acceptable Year of the Lord

Wherever Jesus went, He operated as a man anointed with the Holy Spirit and power, destroying the works of the devil.

> **Acts 10:38 How God anointed Jesus of Nazareth with the Holy Spirit and with power, who went about doing**

good and healing all who were oppressed by the devil, for God was with Him.

If Jesus was healing all who were oppressed by the devil, then it's clear where oppression and sickness comes from – Satan. If sickness came from God then Jesus would have been contradicting the will of the Father by healing those oppressed.

Peculiar Anointings

Let's talk for a moment about some of the peculiar things that Jesus did in His ministry, as led by the Holy Spirit.

- Jesus Heals a Deaf Mute: Jesus put his fingers into a man's ears. Then he spit and touched the man's tongue (Mark 7:32-34).

- Jesus Heals a Blind Man: Jesus took the blind man by the hand and led him out of the town. And when He had spit on his eyes and put His hands on him, He asked him if he saw anything. (Mark 8:22-26).

- Jesus Heals the Man Born Blind: He spat on the ground and made clay with the saliva; and He anointed the eyes of the blind man with the clay. And He said to him, "Go, wash in the pool of Siloam" (John 9:1-7).

Jesus never followed what either man or religion considered normal. He waited four days to go visit Lazarus, instead of healing him before he died. He often put people out of the room or led the sick person outside of town before He healed them.

Smith Wigglesworth, a pioneer of the Pentecostal movement in the early 20th century, was known to do some things considered to be odd. Brother Wigglesworth was the mentor of my mentor, Lester Sumrall. His ministry was one of great power and miracles. The deaf heard, the blind saw and the lame walked. Often he would punch the sick person in the area of their illness or pain and God would miraculously heal them. Obviously, this is not something that can be done in the flesh. There was a false apostle named Todd Bentley who did these types of things in his meetings over the past few years. However, his ministry was exposed as a fraud.

Unbelief

As mighty as the ministry of Jesus was, He could not overcome the unbelief of those who rejected His Word. The anointing upon Jesus was subject to the reception of the people. In Mark's gospel, it was written that Jesus could do no mighty work in His own hometown because of unbelief (Mark 6:1-6).

> **Mark 6:5-6**
> **5 Now He could do no mighty work there, except that He laid His hands on a few sick people and healed them.**
> **6 And He marveled because of their unbelief.**

Further, Jesus would remove those with unbelief or take the person away from their surroundings before He performed a miracle. The passage below shows Jesus taking someone outside of town before ministering to him.

Mark 8:22-23

22 Then He came to Bethsaida; and they brought a blind man to Him, and begged Him to touch him.

23 So He took the blind man by the hand and led him out of the town.

What does this tell us about the anointing? That some places and some people are bad for the anointing. They are quenching forces and need to be removed before the anointing can flow. I have been in some church services where I am certain that if Jesus Himself walked in the door, He wouldn't be able to do any mighty work – just like in His hometown of Nazareth (Mark 6).

The Sin of Familiarity

Along these same lines, there is also what I call, the sin of familiarity. This is what Jesus was dealing with in His hometown. If this can happen with Jesus, then it certainly is a potential problem with us ordinary folk. The only problem is that it's ordinary folk who God uses. It's possible to get to know someone in the flesh so well that you stop drawing upon and receiving the anointing that God has placed in his or her life.

It's very similar to making the transition from co-worker to supervisor on your job. You are used to hanging out with the guys, having lunch with them, complaining about the boss together. Now, you find yourself in a situation where you are their direct supervisor. It can lead to some hard feelings because you can't be that same person. There is now a line, a distinction. To ignore it is to jeopardize the work being done, as well as your position.

Pastors, worship leaders, teachers, elders and all spiritual leaders are just human. God has given them a calling, gifts, and an anointing to use them – in spite of their shortcomings and imperfections. For that reason, it's important that you draw upon that calling, those gifts, and the anointing, without getting hung up on their humanity.

According to your Faith
Jesus often required faith from the folks He healed. "According to your faith" Jesus would often say. Today, the requirement hasn't changed. In fact, faith in God should be easier now than it was when Jesus was upon the earth. Hebrews 9:17 says that a testament is of force after the death of the testator. Jesus was healing people based on the promissory note in His earthly ministry. Now that He has gone to the cross and been resurrected, all of the promises of God are "yes and amen" (2 Corinthians 1:20).

The chart below lists all of the recorded instances of Jesus requiring faith from those who received healing.

Healing	Matt	Mark	Luke	John
Leper in Galilee	8:1-4	1:40-45	5:12-15	
Paralytic (palsy) at Capernaum	9:2-8	2:3-12	5:17-26	
Man with a withered hand in Galilee	12:10-13	3:1-7	6:6-11	
Women with issue of blood (hemorrhaging) healed at Capernaum during first preaching tour through Galilee	9:20-22	5:24-34	8:42-48	

Healing (Cont.)	Matt	Mark	Luke	John
Two blind men at Capernaum (on the northern shore of the Sea of Galilee)	9:27-31			
Man born blind who was outside the Temple at Jerusalem				9:1-12; 35-37
Ten lepers between Samaria and Galilee			17:11-19	
Samaritan leper			17:15-19	
Blind Man Approaching Jericho			18:35-43	
Blind Bartimeaus at Jericho		10:46-52		
Two Blind Men Departing Jericho	20:29-34			

Points for Reflection

- When Jesus came to the earth, He temporarily laid aside the attributes of His deity.

- Jesus was and is 100% God and, at the same time, 100% man.

- Jesus did all of His miracles, while on the earth, by the anointing of the Holy Spirit (Acts 10:38).

- Jesus never fit the religious mold and often did things deemed peculiar when ministering to people.

- As mighty as the ministry of Jesus was, He could not overcome the unbelief of those who rejected His Word. The anointing upon Jesus was subject to the reception of the people.

- In many of the miracles that Jesus performed, the recipient was required to have faith.

Sweat vs. Oil

> **Genesis 3:19 In the sweat of your face you shall eat bread till you return to the ground, for out of it you were taken; for dust you *are,* and to dust you shall return.**

Sweat is a byproduct of the fall of Adam. It was a sign that man now toiled apart from God. Adam had lost the sweetness of God's presence and sweat was a constant reminder. Sweat is symbolic of all of the striving that we do to have our own way. We sweat to fulfill our own agenda in our own strength. Sweat is also used to perform a religious duty without the anointing of the Holy Spirit.

The first Adam failed and consequently operated by the sweat of his brow, but the Second Adam came operating by oil – the anointing of the Holy Spirit (Luke 4:18). Jesus, the Second Adam, was tested just like the first Adam was, but Jesus returned in the power of the Spirit.

> **Luke 4:12-13**
> **13 Now when the devil had ended every temptation, he departed from Him until an opportune time.**
> **14 Then Jesus returned in the power of the Spirit to Galilee, and news of Him went out through all the surrounding region.**

It should be remembered that Jesus did sweat, but that His sweat in the garden was great drops of blood (Luke 22:44). Adam's sweat was the curse of sin, but Jesus' sweat was redemptive – to destroy the curse of being separated from God.

We have been restored to fellowship with God through the blood of Jesus.

There is an interesting prophetic picture of the New Covenant in the Old Testament book of Ezekiel. The prophet speaks of the New Covenant priesthood and likens them to the sons of Zadok (44:15). The name Zadok means "righteous" and they are the priests that remained faithful during a time of apostasy.

Ezekiel's vision showed the sons of Zadok, the priests, coming near to the Lord and ministering to Him.

> **Ezekiel 44:16 "They shall enter My sanctuary, and they shall come near My table to minister to Me, and they shall keep My charge.**

Then the prophet said something interesting; he said that when they enter the inner court that they should not clothe themselves with anything that causes sweat.

> **Ezekiel 17-18 And it shall be, whenever they enter the gates of the inner court… they shall not clothe themselves with *anything that causes* sweat.**

Sweat comes about from the work of the flesh and flesh cannot abide in God's presence. In other words, we cannot work our way into the inner court of His presence. "It is not by might, nor by power, but by My Spirit says the Lord" (Zechariah 4:6).

There is now sweat in God's presence!

What is interesting is that the word "sweat" is only in the Bible three times, and we have already mentioned all three.

1. The garden of Eden when Adam sinned
2. The garden of Gethsemane before Jesus went to the Cross

35

3. Ezekiel's vision of the New Covenant priesthood

In summary of these three usages, sweat is the curse of working apart from God, the blood of Jesus restores us to God and we may now enter His presence only by His grace and without the sweat of our efforts.

Now let's focus on the matter of ministry. Sweat represents man working for God with his own intellect, talent and effort. Oil represents the anointing of the Holy Spirit, which empowers us supernaturally outside of our natural abilities.

Here is a list comparing and contrasting "sweat" with "oil."

Ministry

Sweat	Oil
• Separation from God	• United with God
• Desire	• Anointing
• Hard work	• Calling
• Talent	• Gifting
• Intellect	• Obedience
• Education	• Impartation
• Pride	• Knowledge
	• Humility

True ministry can only be done through the anointing of the Holy Spirit. Jesus said, "That which is born of the flesh is flesh" (John 3:3). In other words, a person cannot start off with self-empowered ministry and expect God to come along afterwards and bless it with His anointing. Jesus went on to say, "That which is born of the Spirit is Spirit." What He was saying is that if you want the anointing of God on what you're doing, you must start off in the Spirit.

When I was pastoring in Indiana, there was a man in the church who wanted to be a preacher. He even completed a two-year Bible college program. The only problem was that in spite of his desire and his efforts, there was no anointing on him when he spoke. The man had a pretty good job in restaurant management, but decided one day that he was going into full-time ministry. He resigned his job and waited for the doors to open. Presumption can often masquerade as the Spirit's leading. When we act presumptuously in the flesh, we, in effect, think we have "painted God into a corner" where He "must" bless us. Sometimes, there are very hard lessons to learn in the Lord's work. This was one of those times for this gentleman. After several months of closed doors, the Lord had mercy on him and he was able to get re-employment and provide for his family again.

Now, while one cannot begin in the flesh and end in the Spirit, it is possible to begin in the Spirit and end up in the flesh. Perhaps I should clarify my first statement; when I say that one cannot begin in the flesh and end in the Spirit, I mean unless there is repentance. A person can repent and get in the Spirit, but otherwise, the flesh never converts. Sweat will not become oil at some point.

It is also important to stay in our anointing and not deviate. Perhaps someone else has an anointing that we want, so the temptation is to copy them and expect the same results. That doesn't work! Many of the healing evangelists of the twentieth century wanted to be great teachers, but that wasn't their calling. As a consequence of some of them forcing their way into the teaching role, they fell victim to heresies. John Alexander Dowie (1847-1907) and William Branham (1909-1965) are two prime examples. Dowie believed that he was Elijah and Branham eventually denied the Trinity and believed that he was one of the two witnesses of Revelation.

When a person forces himself into a role that God has not ordained, bad results will occur. The same was true of men in the Bible. Consider Saul; in 1 Samuel 13, when he was instructed to wait on Samuel the Prophet/Priest, he instead got ahead of

God and forced himself into the role of priest. He presumed and allowed presumption to imitate the anointing.

The following verses are the exchange that Samuel had with Saul afterwards.

> **1 Samuel 13:11-12 (KJV)**
> **11 And Samuel said, What hast thou done? And Saul said, Because I saw that the people were scattered from me, and that thou camest not within the days appointed, and that the Philistines gathered themselves together at Michmash;**
> **12 Therefore said I, The Philistines will come down now upon me to Gilgal, and I have not made supplication unto the Lord: I forced myself therefore, and offered a burnt offering.**
> **13 And Samuel said to Saul, Thou hast done foolishly...**

Three things stand out in this passage:

1. Saul was more concerned with being popular with the people than obeying God (v 11).
2. Saul forced himself into a role that he was not called into (v 12).
3. Samuel accurately defined these actions as "foolishness" (v 13).

Saul's foolish acts cost him the kingdom. I'm always amazed at how we frequently take the anointing for granted and as a consequence do foolish things that strip the anointing from us. This is not to say that we cannot have the anointing restored, but in Saul's case, his rebellion cost him and his house forever. It has been said that a man of God can lose in 20 minutes what took him 20 years to build. Guarding the heart is a daily requirement.

Proverbs 4:23 Keep your heart with all diligence, for out of it *spring* the issues of life.

Martha and Mary

Another example of sweat vs. oil in the Bible is found in the story of Martha and Mary, in the New Testament.

Luke 10:38-42

38 Now it happened as they went that He entered a certain village; and a certain woman named Martha welcomed Him into her house.

39 And she had a sister called Mary, who also sat at Jesus' feet and heard His word.

40 But Martha was distracted with much serving, and she approached Him and said, "Lord, do You not care that my sister has left me to serve alone? Therefore tell her to help me."

41 And Jesus answered and said to her, "Martha, Martha, you are worried and troubled about many things.

42 But one thing is needed, and Mary has chosen that good part, which will not be taken away from her."

As we compare and contrast Martha and Mary and how they interacted with Jesus, we can quickly see how Martha symbolized service with a sweat and Mary service with oil.

Martha - Sweat	Mary - Oil
• Received Jesus (v. 38) • Outwardly served Jesus – distracted with much serving (v. 40) • Prayed selfishly to Jesus ("Lord, do you not care...") (v. 40) • Worried & Troubled (v. 41)	• Spent time with Jesus sitting at His feet (v. 39) • Heard His Word (v. 39) • Wasn't distracted and worried (v. 40) • Had her priorities right (v. 42)

Mary's focus was on the Vertical – her fellowship with God, while Martha's focus was on the Horizontal – what she could do to serve Him in her own effort. The oil of anointing is always an outflow of time spent with the Lord. Martha thought that the extreme measures of service would be pleasing to the Lord and that He would correct Mary of her lack thereof. But her service was the sweat of the flesh, which can never please God.

In fact, the book of Exodus tells us that the holy anointing oil shall not be poured upon the flesh.

> **Exodus 30:31-32**
> **31 And you shall speak to the children of Israel, saying: This shall be a holy anointing oil to Me throughout your generations.**
> **32 It shall not be poured on man's flesh; nor shall you make *any other* like it, according to its composition. It *is* holy, *and* it shall be holy to you.**

The flesh can be very outwardly religious, but it cannot have the oil of His presence. The Spirit and the flesh are very much opposites with completely different agendas. They fight against one another, as Paul explained to the Galatians.

> **Galatians 5:16-17**
> **16 I say then: Walk in the Spirit, and you shall not fulfill the lust of the flesh.**
> **17 For the flesh lusts against the Spirit, and the Spirit against the flesh; and these are contrary to one another, so that you do not do the things that you wish.**

This is how the Amplified Bible translates the latter part of verse 17: *For these are antagonistic to each other [continually withstanding and in conflict with each other], so that you are not free but are prevented from doing what you desire to do.* There is a continual conflict between the oil of the Spirit and the sweat of the flesh. Until a believer gets free from the sweat of the flesh, he will not be able to flow in the oil of the Spirit. Romans 8:8 says that "They that are in the flesh cannot please God."

The problem is that religion celebrates the work of the flesh. In fact, it parades it to the people as the standard that pleases God. "Just do this, that and the other and you will have the favor of God." Since the fall of Adam in the garden, man has been trying to work and merit his way back to God.

Too often, it is only after we fail in the flesh that we are usable to God. Consider this list of examples of men who failed on their own before allowing God to work through them:

- **Abraham** (fathered Ishmael trying to fulfill God's promise in the flesh)

- **Jacob** (tried to get ahead through deception until a wrestling match with God)

- **Moses** (killed the Egyptian thinking that Israel would follow him)

- **Jonah** (fled the opposite direction from God's will until God intervened)

- **Peter** (denied the Lord Jesus three times before being filled with the Spirit)

41

- **Paul** (a devout religious leader who denied Jesus until his conversion)

God chooses the weak and the foolish to confound the mighty and the wise (1 Corinthians 1:27). He does not call the qualified but qualifies the called. The Lord will not allow us to trust in the arm of the flesh. His purposes can only be accomplished by His anointing upon vessels that are humble and yielded.

Points for Reflection

- Sweat is a byproduct of the fall of Adam. It was a sign that man now toiled apart from God.

- The first Adam failed and consequently operated by the sweat of his brow, but the Second Adam came operating by oil – the anointing of the Holy Spirit.

- While one cannot begin in the flesh and end in the Spirit (unless there is repentance), it is possible to begin in the Spirit and end up in the flesh.

- It is important to stay in the calling and anointing that God has given you and not to deviate.

- Martha is a good example of sweat and Mary is a good example of oil (Luke 10:38-42).

- The Bible is filled with many examples of those who tried and failed in the flesh before the succeeded by doing it God's way.

Case Studies from the Bible

I have always been fascinated with certain men in the Bible who had mighty a anointing from God, even though their character was less than stellar at times. I have listed a few of them out below. My purpose is not to focus on their failures, but the keys to the anointing in their lives.

Samson

Let's first look at the life of Samson (Judges 13-16). He was a judge for 20 years over Israel. He had a Nazarite vow. The Nazarite vow is taken by individuals who have voluntarily dedicated themselves to God. The Hebrew word *nazir*, simply means "to be separated or consecrated." A New Testament parallel to the Nazarite vow can be found in Romans 12:

> **Romans 12:1 I beseech you therefore, brethren, by the mercies of God, that you present your bodies a living sacrifice, holy, acceptable to God, which is your reasonable service.**

The Old Testament vow included abstaining from strong drink, from shaving or cutting the hair, and from contact with a dead body. Samson possessed extraordinary physical strength. Most drawings of Samson depict him as having very large muscles. However, this is not likely the case. The Philistines worked very hard to find the secret to his strength. If he had large muscles, there would have been no secret.

Samson, however, had a problem with flirting with the world. This led to him busing the anointing of God in his life. Three times in Judges 14 and 15 we read, "The Spirit of the Lord came upon Samson" (14:6, 19; 15:14). He was doing mighty works by the anointing of God. But Satan's assignment was in motion to bring him down.

Judges 16:4-5
4 Now afterward it happened that he loved a woman in the Valley of Sorek, whose name was Delilah.
5 And the lords of the Philistines came up to her and said to her, "Entice him and find out where his great strength lies, and by what means we may overpower him, that we may bind him and afflict him.

There is an all-out attack from Satan against those with the anointing of God on their lives. He comes enticing God's servants with the three G's:

1. **The Glory**
2. **The Gold**
3. **The Girls**

In Judges 16, we read once again of three supernatural feats, only this time it does not say. "The Spirit of the Lord came upon Him." The anointing had departed and all that remained was the lingering Spirit for the purpose of repentance (see Psalm 51:10-12).

Samson was mistaking the Holy Spirit's lingering presence, for the purpose of repentance, for the anointing for the supernatural. He was squandering God's holy presence on feats that were more suited for a sideshow!

Some have regressed to the point that they don't even know the Holy Spirit's anointing has lifted from their life. They have been too busy amusing themselves with the attractions of this world. One day Samson came to a rude awakening:

> **Judges 16:20-21**
> **20 And she said, "The Philistines are upon you, Samson!" So he awoke from his sleep, and said, "I will go out as before, at other times, and shake myself free!" But he did not know that the LORD had departed from him.**
> **21 Then the Philistines took him and put out his eyes, and brought him down to Gaza. They bound him with bronze fetters, and he became a grinder in the prison.**

Samson presumed he would go out and shake himself as before and the power of God would come. When the anointing is gone, the old formulas don't work!

Just because a person is anointed, he should never begin to think that he is something special, incapable of falling. Paul wrote, "Let him who thinks he stands, take heed lest he fall" (1 Corinthians 10:12).

They put out Samson's eyes. The losing wrestler in the Greek wrestling matches Paul wrote about in Ephesians 6:12 had his eyes gouged out. There was no discernment left in Samson's life, now he had lost his physical eyes as well.

He was bound and made a grinder in the prison. He had gone from being a mighty champion for God to becoming a prisoner to his enemies. However, in the end, Samson had his strength restored and the anointing of God came back on his life for one final demonstration of God's power.

> **Judges 16:28-30**
> **28 Then Samson called to the Lord, saying, "O Lord God, remember me, I pray! Strengthen me, I pray, just this once, O God, that I may with one blow take vengeance on the Philistines for my two eyes!"**
> **29 And Samson took hold of the two middle pillars which supported the temple, and he braced himself against them, one on his right and the other on his left.**
> **30 Then Samson said, "Let me die with the Philistines!" And he pushed with all his might, and the temple fell on the lords and all the people who were in it. So the dead that he killed at his death were more than he had killed in his life.**

King Saul

Saul is another interesting case when it comes to the anointing. He was chosen to be king after Israel rejected God as their king. He was anointed to be king by the prophet Samuel.

Saul was filled with natural ability:

> **1 Samuel 9:2 And he had a choice and handsome son whose name was Saul. There was not a more**

handsome person than he among the children of Israel. From his shoulders upward he was taller than any of the people.

Sometimes it may be too easy for those with talent and good looks. The anointing could perhaps be taken for granted and deemed unnecessary. Saul began his reign over Israel successfully. But ultimately, rebellion was his downfall. He spared when God said to spare not.

> **1 Samuel 15:22-23**
> **22 So Samuel said: "Has the Lord as great delight in burnt offerings and sacrifices, as in obeying the voice of the Lord? Behold, to obey is better than sacrifice, and to heed than the fat of rams.**
> **23 For rebellion is as the sin of witchcraft, and stubbornness is as iniquity and idolatry. Because you have rejected the word of the Lord, He also has rejected you from being king."**

When one experiences success in the ministry, it is tempting to take the anointing for granted. It can be rationalized that God expects me to take some for myself – even if He has instructed not to do so.

Obedience to God is the key to any anointing. When we feel that we are too big to obey in the small areas, we have been deceived by pride. Saul, through his rebellion, had opened a door to witchcraft in his life that can be seen throughout his remaining years. At times, a young David would have to come and play the harp and the anointing on David's ministry would drive away the demons that haunted Saul.

Ultimately, Saul became jealous and threatened by David. The women sang, "Saul has slain his thousands, and David his tens of thousands" (1 Samuel 18:7). This infuriated Saul. He tried to kill David at least 12 times.

> **When the anointing is gone, a spirit of competition and jealousy will enter.**

If the church or ministry that you are under begins to operate out of competition, beware! If the leader is constantly feeling threatened by other ministries and churches, beware! When someone is operating in the anointing of God, there is a spirit of love at work.

There is also an interesting thing that occurred in the life of Saul that is worth mentioning, as it relates to the anointing. After Saul had been rejected as king and had made several attempts to kill David, he came among the sons of the prophets, and he himself began to prophesy.

> **1 Samuel 19:23 So he went there to Naioth in Ramah. Then the Spirit of God was upon him also, and he went on and prophesied until he came to Naioth in Ramah.**

This shows that there was still gifting in Saul and when he got around the anointing of God with the prophets, he was able to prophesy. This highlights the need to not only examine the gifts of a person, but the fruit of his life also. This is different than simply being human and imperfect. Saul's life was in rebellion to God. Those who reject God's ways and seek their own authority should not be followed.

Ultimately, Saul drove himself to insanity through his lack of repentance.

King David

The Bible says that King David was "a man after God's own heart" (Acts 13:22). He was chosen by God to lead His people after the rebellion of Saul. He was not perfect by any stretch, but his heart was contrite before the Lord. Let's first look at his anointing to be king.

> **1 Samuel 16:1, 6-7, 10-13**
> **1** Now the Lord said to Samuel, "How long will you mourn for Saul, seeing I have rejected him from reigning over Israel? Fill your horn with oil, and go; I am sending you to Jesse the Bethlehemite. For I have provided Myself a king among his sons."
>
> **6** So it was, when they came, that he looked at Eliab and said, "Surely the Lord's anointed is before Him!"
> **7** But the Lord said to Samuel, "Do not look at his appearance or at his physical stature, because I have refused him. For the Lord does not see as man sees; for man looks at the outward appearance, but the Lord looks at the heart."
>
> **10** Thus Jesse made seven of his sons pass before Samuel. And Samuel said to Jesse, "The Lord has not chosen these."
> **11** And Samuel said to Jesse, "Are all the young men here?" Then he said, "There remains yet the youngest, and there he is, keeping the sheep." And Samuel said

to Jesse, "Send and bring him. For we will not sit down till he comes here."

12 So he sent and brought him in. Now he was ruddy, with bright eyes, and good-looking. And the Lord said, "Arise, anoint him; for this is the one!"

13 Then Samuel took the horn of oil and anointed him in the midst of his brothers; and the Spirit of the Lord came upon David from that day forward. So Samuel arose and went to Ramah.

David was the youngest and least likely of Jesse's eight sons. He was out tending the sheep, and likely worshipping Yahweh. David was anointed with the harp and song. During his time, David wrote approximately half of the 150 psalms in the Bible. There is so much to talk about when one does a character study on the life of David. But let's touch on a few of the areas related to the anointing.

The anointing is not based on the outer appearance, but on the heart (1 Samuel 16:7). God had Samuel pass on seven of Jesse's sons, even though they "looked the part." Remember, Saul also looked the part, but his heart was rebellious.

David was willing to be used by the Lord by serving Saul, even though he had been anointed king. He became Saul's armorbearer (1 Samuel 16:21). This revealed David's servant heart. Jesus said that the greatest among us would be our servant (Matthew 23:11).

David would not touch or come against God's anointed (1 Chronicles 16:22). "God's anointed" was God's delegated authority, which in this case, was Saul. Even though Saul had been rejected and David had been anointed, he was still in authority. David did not usurp authority and take in the flesh what God had given him. Saul tried to kill David at least 12 times, but when David had the chance to kill Saul, he would not. When God has called and anointed you, he will open the door.

Proverbs 18:16 A man's gift makes room for him, and brings him before great men.

Psalm 75:5-6 (KJV)
5 Lift not up your horn on high: speak not with a stiff neck.
6 For promotion cometh neither from the east, nor from the west, nor from the south.

David was about 15 years old when Samuel anointed him king. He did not take the throne until the age of 30. In the beginning, Saul loved David, but it turned to hatred through jealousy. The women of Israel sang, "Saul has slain his thousands, And David his ten thousands" (1 Samuel 18:7).

After ascending the throne, David's first concern was to restore the Ark – God's glory – to Zion (2 Samuel 6). David danced before the Lord with all his might as they brought back the Ark of the Covenant. He was not concerned with appearing dignified. His wife, Michal, looked from the window of their palace and was indignant that her husband the king would act like a fool in public.

1 Samuel 16:20-23
20 Then David returned to bless his household. And Michal the daughter of Saul came out to meet David,

and said, "How glorious was the king of Israel today, uncovering himself today in the eyes of the maids of his servants, as one of the base fellows shamelessly uncovers himself!"

21 So David said to Michal, "It was before the Lord, who chose me instead of your father and all his house, to appoint me ruler over the people of the Lord, over Israel. Therefore I will play music before the Lord.

22 And I will be even more undignified than this, and will be humble in my own sight. But as for the maidservants of whom you have spoken, by them I will be held in honor."

23 Therefore Michal the daughter of Saul had no children to the day of her death.

Basically, David told her, "You ain't seen nothing yet!" He was a man after God's own heart and was willing to be undignified for the glory of the Lord. As for Michal, she was barren from that day forward. This is a lesson for all that grieve the Spirit with their persistence on being dignified in the house of the Lord.

David was not perfect. He failed God but was not removed because of his repentance (2 Samuel 11, Psalm 51). We all know what happened with David and Bathsheba. He committed adultery and had her husband killed in battle. To make matters worse, David harbored his sin for two years until Nathan the prophet confronted him with "Thou art the man." (2 Samuel 12:7). There were repercussions for David's sin (the sword never departed from his house), but God restored him and continued to use him after repentance.

David was a worshipper. He set the Ark of the Covenant in a tent and it remained there for 40 years. The only sacrifices, after the inauguration, were the sacrifices of praise before the Ark night and day. This is known as the Tabernacle of David and is prophesied to be restored in the last days (Acts 15:16).

Before his fall, Lucifer was called "the anointed cherub" (Ezekiel 28:14). He was the worship leader before the throne in heaven. One day, Lucifer decided he wanted to be the one worshipped. As a result, he was cast out of heaven. As God's anointed, it is important to remain the worshipper and not seek the worship of men.

Elijah

The Bible says that Elijah was a man subject to the same nature and passions as us, but he prayed earnestly and fervently (James 5:16-18). Elijah saw some mighty miracles in his ministry as prophet. At times, he was fearless, but at other times he was cowardly. Just like us.

Right after calling down fire from heaven in a standoff against the prophets of Baal (1 Kings 18), Elijah fled in fear from Jezebel due to her threat to kill him. He sat down under the Juniper tree and asked God to kill him. He felt like he was all alone with no one else serving the Lord.

My point here is that being anointed does not immunize you from fears, anxieties, pressures and depression. Elijah, and other prophets experienced all of that and more. The prophet Jeremiah felt like God had deceived him and he vowed to never speak in God's name again. However, the Word of God was stored up in his heart and began to burn like a fire (Jeremiah 20:7-9).

While under the juniper tree, Elijah also learned a valuable lesson about hearing God. There was a strong wind, then there was an earthquake, after that a fire. But the Lord was not in these very forceful, outward occurrences. Finally, there was a still small voice – the voice of the Holy Spirit (1 Kings 19:11-13). Too many times, we look for outward signs or booming voices from heaven. God speaks in the inward man with a still small voice. We need to be listening.

Elisha - Apprenticeship

Learning to flow in the anointing also involves apprenticeship. Consider the ministry of Elisha and how he served the prophet Elijah. Elisha served Elijah faithfully. He was known throughout Israel as the one who poured water over Elijah's hands (1 Kings 3:11).

God was preparing Elisha to receive the double portion of the anointing. It is hard to find a faithful man, but God found one in Elisha. Many will serve in a ministry, up to the point where they think they can launch out on their own – at the expense of their mentor, taking his sheep or resources. But Elisha stayed true to the end and God rewarded him.

Three times in 2 Kings chapter two, Elisha tells his mentor, "As the Lord lives, and as your soul lives, I will not leave you!" Upon seeing such faithfulness, Elijah asked him what he would like for him to do for him. Elisha said, "Please let a double portion of your spirit be upon me."

2 Kings 2:10-15

10 So he said, "You have asked a hard thing. Nevertheless, if you see me when I am taken from you, it shall be so for you; but if not, it shall not be so."

11 Then it happened, as they continued on and talked, that suddenly a chariot of fire appeared with horses of fire, and separated the two of them; and Elijah went up by a whirlwind into heaven.

12 And Elisha saw it, and he cried out, "My father, my father, the chariot of Israel and its horsemen!" So he saw him no more. And he took hold of his own clothes and tore them into two pieces.

13 He also took up the mantle of Elijah that had fallen from him, and went back and stood by the bank of the Jordan.

14 Then he took the mantle of Elijah that had fallen from him, and struck the water, and said, "Where is the Lord God of Elijah?" And when he also had struck the water, it was divided this way and that; and Elisha crossed over.

15 Now when the sons of the prophets who were from Jericho saw him, they said, "The spirit of Elijah rests on Elisha." And they came to meet him, and bowed to the ground before him.

This is why you see a similarity of anointing on a person who has served under another. God has divine connections for each of us by placing certain people in our lives. Don't be so quick to move on until the Holy Spirit releases you. You just might be in line for a double portion of the anointing.

Points for Reflection

- There are several examples found in the Word of God of men who had less than stellar character, but had a mighty anointing of God upon their lives.

- Samson was mistaking the Holy Spirit's lingering presence, for the purpose of repentance, for the anointing for the supernatural.

- Obedience to God is the key to any anointing. When we feel that we are too big to obey in the small areas, we have been deceived by pride.

- When the anointing is gone, a spirit of competition and jealousy will enter.

- The anointing is not based on the outer appearance, but on the heart (1 Samuel 16:7).

- There will always be a similarity of anointing on a person who has served under another.

My Personal Experience

Over the years, I have learned many things about the anointing of the Holy Spirit that I didn't know in my earlier years of ministry. I still have so much to learn. But we have the best teacher ever – the Holy Spirit. In this section, I will attempt to convey certain things I've learned. I'm always hesitant to preach or write with a lot of "I's" involved. I never want to draw attention to myself or base anything solely off of my personal experience. However, it's also important to share the things that we learn along the way in an effort to help others. **These points are my personal experience and yours may vary.**

There are some things that you cannot learn in a book; it requires time and experience. The more time that you spend operating in the anointing of the Holy Spirit, the more you learn how to be led by the Spirit.

Below are a few things that I have learned over the years.

Relax and know that He is God

> **Psalm 46:10 Be still (Heb. "relax") and know that I am God.**

Stressing about if, how and when the Holy Spirit will move is a quenching force. We just need to allow Him to have His way. Refuse to allow yourself to get under pressure. Sometimes people want you to "perform." It is the Holy Spirit who does the work; we are just vessels for Him to flow through. During the healing revivals of the 1950's, various evangelists would perform under pressure because of the enormous expectations that had been created. This caused works of the flesh and even familiar spirits to be in play.

Don't try to do more than the anointing. When the anointing of the Holy Spirit lifts, don't keep going in the flesh.

It's not about feelings.

I have prayed for people and thought, as I was praying, "I feel nothing… this person isn't getting anything," only to have them tell me several days later that they were completely healed.

So, while the anointing is generally something you can feel (not emotionally feel, but spiritually feel), there are times when you are simply operating by faith and trusting God.

2 Corinthians 5:7 For we walk by faith, not by sight.

Hearing the voice of the Spirit is easier than I thought.

Jesus said in John 10:4-5 that His sheep know His voice and the voice of a stranger they will not follow. This is true "stranger danger." It's important to note that Jesus used the word "know" when it came to His voice. We know with our spirit not our mind. Our mind may or may not understand, but through His voice, we know in our spirit.

The Holy Spirit most often speaks in a still small voice, just like with Elijah in 1 Kings 19. I don't second-guess what I hear nearly as much as what I used to. There is a peace in knowing that the Holy Spirit is speaking. More than learning to hear God's voice, it has been a process of learning to tune out all the other voices (rationalization, fear, pride, doubt, etc.).

The Holy Spirit speaks to us intuitively in our spirits. In other words, you simply get a knowing that doesn't come from your mind. It is not based on facts or information previously presented. You may not understand it, but you know it. This happens frequently under the anointing.

> **1 Corinthians 2:14 But the natural man does not receive the things of the Spirit of God, for they are foolishness to him; nor can he know them, because they are spiritually discerned.**

> **Romans 8:14 For as many as are led by the Spirit of God, these are sons of God.**

When people come forward for prayer, they generally line up next to one another. When I start praying for people, the Holy Spirit always shows me who to go to first. No one should think that they are being passed over. Just stay in the Spirit and be patient. We all want what is from the Holy Spirit, not man.

One question that I get quite frequently is, "Why do you stare at me all the time when you preach?" I usually respond with, "I don't know what you're talking about." When the anointing is present, you do things physically that you don't always have self-awareness of. Perhaps it is a way that the Lord gets someone's attention.

My prayers are different – more potent – when I'm under the anointing.

This is difficult to explain to someone who's never experienced the anointing of the Holy Spirit. By the way, you don't have to be a preacher to have an anointing. In a funny way, it's almost like when Clark Kent steps into the phone booth and comes out Super Man. The point is, you have a certain boldness and faith when you're operating under the anointing that goes beyond the normal. And ultimately, there is a power in demonstration to heal and deliver. This is all for the purpose of glorifying Jesus and restoring God's children. There is no self-acclaim associated with the anointing.

Another thing that I have noticed is that I become incredibly focused when under the anointing of the Holy Spirit. This is true whether I am preaching or praying for people. The worst thing to do when someone is under the anointing is to start waving at them to interrupt and get their attention. Unless the building is on fire, don't break the flow.

God confirms His Word.

When I seek God on what He wants me to preach on, He always speaks to me a particular topic. I then record notes as the Holy Spirit speaks to me over the course of several days. I use these notes to prepare the material; when doing so, I always focus on three things:

- Is the material *preachable*?
- Is the material *practical*?
- Is the material *prayable*?

Let me explain. First, is it "preachable?" I know the areas where God has given me a strong anointing to preach. It's not just the content, but how the content is delivered. I will prepare the material in a way that matches my delivery style.

Second, is it practical? In other words, does the message translate into people's everyday lives? It's one thing to be inspired at church, but the key to victory is being able to live by the Word of God to overcome life's problems.

Lastly, the message needs to be "prayable." If the sermon is about the antichrist, having an altar call for healing may have lesser results than if the message was on the topic of healing or faith. Romans 10:17 says that faith comes from hearing the Word of God. The Lord wants to confirm His Word with signs following.

> **Mark 16:20 And they went out and preached everywhere, the Lord working with them and confirming the word through the accompanying signs.**

Don't worry about listing all your problems!

I can't begin to tell you how many people come forward for one area and the Holy Spirit will have me pray for something different. But in the process, He takes care of their original problem. For instance, someone may come forward for healing in their leg and I will pray over them to be delivered from anger. When they get back to their seat, the person realizes that their leg is healed. And their anger is gone too. 1 Peter 5:7 says to cast all of your care upon the Lord.

There are times when I feel led to stop and ask, "What do you want Jesus to do for you?" And other times, I pray as directed by the Holy Spirit. The key, if you need prayer, is that you keep your eyes on Jesus.

Stay in your anointing.

The temptation is always there to do things just because someone else is doing them or because it's the new craze. Just abide in the anointing that God has developed in you. In other words, "function in your unction."

There are churches that place themselves into certain "camps." This is true even of many non-denominational churches. These camps generally center on a certain famous preacher or a particular teaching. There are faith camps, doctrine camps, prosperity camps, personality camps, etc. Our focus at The River is to be a Jesus camp.

An example of *not* staying in your anointing is when an evangelist who is used in signs and wonders tries to become a teacher. The only problem is that if there's not a calling and anointing to teach, there can be a propensity for error. Some of the greatest evangelists in history were shipwrecked with false doctrine because they stepped out of their anointing.

More to Learn
There is much more that could be shared from learning experiences, and there is still more that must be learned. Sometimes we are not ready to receive what the Holy Spirit wants to show.

> **John 16:12-15**
> **12 "I still have many things to say to you, but you cannot bear them now.**

13 However, when He, the Spirit of truth, has come, He will guide you into all truth; for He will not speak on His own authority, but whatever He hears He will speak; and He will tell you things to come.

14 He will glorify Me, for He will take of what is Mine and declare it to you.

15 All things that the Father has are Mine. Therefore I said that He will take of Mine and declare it to you.

Points for Reflection

There are some things that you cannot learn in a book; it requires time and experience.

Don't try to do more than the anointing. When the anointing of the Holy Spirit lifts, don't keep going in the flesh.

The Holy Spirit most often speaks in a still small voice, just like with Elijah in 1 Kings 19.

Fresh Oil

The Lord never does anything stale, but instead fresh. His anointing cannot be duplicated from the last meeting we attended. Sometimes we run off to a conference and get in God's anointing. The songs are awesome, the preaching is awesome, and the prayer time is awesome. We come home and the first Sunday back, we want to duplicate everything we experienced. We sing the same songs, preach the same message, and call for prayer in the same way. But there is a notable and conspicuous absence of the Holy Spirit's anointing. That's because we must seek God for a fresh anointing.

Psalm 92:10 I have been anointed with fresh oil.

It has been said that the last seven words of a dying church are:

"That's the way we've always done it."

It's amazing that some groups feel like they cannot fall prey to the temptation of the traditions of men. I've been part of the Pentecostal/Charismatic community for over 30 years and I have seen countless traditions of men in practice – while at the same time, we were putting ourselves on a pedestal above traditional denominations. Often, the last person to notice is the one, or the group, that is caught up in tradition.

We must guard our hearts against this by continually examining *why* we do things. Do we do them because that's just the way we have seen it done our whole lives or because that's what the Word says? Sometimes we think it's the latter, but upon examination, it is the former – because that's the way it was learned by example.

"Today, Lord, expose all of my traditions of men that keep me from the power of Your Word in my life and ministry."

Diversity/ Sameness

Every person is different. Every church is different. As unique vessels, not only does God want to do things in a fresh way each time, but also in a unique manner. In other words, you can't just copy someone and expect the same results. A church cannot just follow another churches' program and expect the same growth. One thing for sure about the Holy Spirit – He likes variety.

> **1 Corinthians 12:4-7**
> **4 There are diversities of gifts, but the same Spirit.**
> **5 There are differences of ministries, but the same Lord.**
> **6 And there are diversities of activities, but it is the same God who works all in all.**
> **7 But the manifestation of the Spirit is given to each one for the profit of all.**

There is a diversity of gifts, ministries and activities – but the same God. How do you know when it's the Holy Spirit? Your spirit bears witness (not the mention that it lines up to the Word of God). There is diversity but sameness. Two people can do things completely different, but if under the anointing, get the same result.

As individuals, we must be unique, as God intended us to be. When the Holy Spirit inspired the Gospels, He used four different men to give the accounts of Jesus. They each described the same events, but the stories read differently. That's because even though each Gospel was 100% inspired by the Holy Spirit, He used each one's individuality and uniqueness. The same is true today.

Further, as a church, God wants each body of believers to be a unique local expression of the body of Christ. You can't copy some other church and expect the freedom of the Holy Spirit to be present. God will give you your own style of worship, your own outreach ministries, etc. You can learn from other people and other churches. They can impart into you through their gifts and anointing. This is because of the sameness of Spirit. But you cannot afford to lose the diversity that makes the body what the body is supposed to be.

New Wineskins

Jesus taught the principle of always being adaptable to the Spirit. He used the parable of the wineskins to illustrate this principle.

> **Luke 5:37-38**
> **37 And no one puts new wine into old wineskins; or else the new wine will burst the wineskins and be spilled, and the wineskins will be ruined.**
> **38 But new wine must be put into new wineskins, and both are preserved.**

Wine is a symbol of the Holy Spirit. New wine needs a new wineskin because as the new wine expands during the fermentation process, it stretches the wineskin. An old wineskin will burst under the pressure of new wine.

Some Christians have been old wineskins for so long that they don't even realize that the new wine is no longer present. This has nothing to do with someone's chronological age or his or her spiritual age. It has to do with one's open mindedness and willingness to follow the Holy Spirit's leading.

I frequently use music as an example when discussing this subject. It is something that we can all relate to and typically, we each have our own preference as it relates to style. I will now oversimplify this by showing how one's age gives bias toward music style.

- Older people may feel very strongly about the classical hymns. This is because they have gone to war with those hymns in the trials of life and they help them to recall God's wondrous working power.
- Middle-aged people, if in the church long enough, may have an affinity toward worship songs from the 1980s and 90s. This style was once cutting edge; it came about during a period of time when it was hard for churches to break away from the hymnal.
- Younger people typically respond better to current music styles. Some of these styles are very appropriate for worship, while others are not.

Again, the above is a stereotype and oversimplifies the subject. But as an example, it helps to see that certain biases can develop that may not necessarily originate from the Holy Spirit, but instead our own likes and dislikes.

There is a beautiful movement of the Holy Spirit in the area of worship music. New and fresh worship music is being birthed by the Spirit in the hearts of a new generation. An example of this type of worship is the ministry Hillsong. Artists such as Matt Redmond and Chris Tomlin are also good examples.

Worship music has two objectives. Obviously, the first and most important is to worship God. But the second is also important because it has direct impact on the first – that is, to speak to people's hearts and draw them into worship of the Father.

Two Purposes of Worship Music

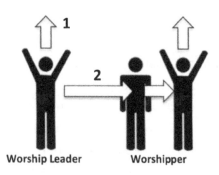

Worship Leader   Worshipper

As it relates to fresh oil and the anointing, the worship leader should seek God and get songs fresh from God's presence. This may include some of the older songs, but should not neglect songs that speak into the hearts of the younger generation.

Prayer

Heavenly Father, we surrender all to You. Our desire is that You would use us for the glory of Your Son Jesus. There are needs and hurts all around and we do not possess the help that they need, outside of You. Flow through us Your precious anointing to minister into their lives. Increase the anointing of God upon our lives. Manifest Your presence in this church through signs and wonders and various miracles. Heal the brokenhearted and set the captives free.

In Jesus' Name – amen.

Points for Reflection

The Lord never does anything stale, but instead fresh.

We must guard our hearts against this by continually examining why we do things.

Two people can do things completely different, but if under the anointing, get the same result.

There is a diversity of gifts, ministries and activities – but the same God.

Manifestation Gifts of the Holy Spirit

In my book "The Fullness of the Spirit" I break down each of the nine gifts of the Spirit, as listed in 1 Corinthians chapter 12. This chapter is an expanded version of that material.

In order to walk in the supernatural anointing of God, it is imperative that we understand the various gifts of the Spirit. These gifts, or manifestations, are a big part of the operation of the anointing.

To start with, there are more than nine gifts listed in the New Testament. But there are only nine that are defined as manifestations. Here are the New Testament gifts listed, by category:

There are the *Ministry* gifts of the Spirit (Ephesians 4:11):
1. Apostle
2. Prophet
3. Evangelist
4. Pastor
5. Teacher

There are the *Manifestation* gifts of the Spirit (1 Corinthians 12:7-11):
1. Prophecy

2. Tongues
3. Interpretation of Tongues
4. Word of Wisdom
5. Word of Knowledge
6. Discerning of Spirits
7. Working of Miracles
8. Healings
9. Faith

There are *Motivational* gifts of the Spirit (Romans 12:6-8, 1 Corinthians 12:28):
1. Giving
2. Exhortation
3. Administration
4. Helps
5. Mercy

Note: Faith, Prophecy and Teaching are listed more than once.

Presently, we will focus on the manifestation gifts of the Spirit.

> **1 Corinthians 12:4-11**
> **4 There are diversities of gifts, but the same Spirit.**
> **5 There are differences of ministries, but the same Lord.**
> **6 And there are diversities of activities, but it is the same God who works all in all.**
> **7 But the manifestation of the Spirit is given to each one for the profit of all:**

8 for to one is given the <u>word of wisdom</u> through the Spirit, to another the <u>word of knowledge</u> through the same Spirit,
9 to another <u>faith</u> by the same Spirit, to another <u>gifts of healings</u> by the same Spirit,
10 to another the <u>working of miracles</u>, to another <u>prophecy</u>, to another <u>discerning of spirits</u>, to another <u>different kinds of tongues</u>, to another the <u>interpretation of tongues</u>.
11 But one and the same Spirit works all these things, distributing to each one individually as He wills.

I want to draw your attention to two words in this passage: *diversities* and *same* (found in verses 4, 5 and 6). Diversity and Sameness will flow at the same time when the anointing is present. These two words are antonyms in the natural but synonyms in the Spirit. In other words, we all function a little differently (diversity), but it's the same Holy Spirit that is anointing us. Don't try to copy other people. Function in the unction that God has given you.

For the purpose of understanding how these gifts flow together, I have grouped the nine gifts into three categories:

1. Gifts that Reveal something – the Revelation Gifts
2. Gifts that Say something – the Vocal Gifts
3. Gifts that Do something – the Power Gifts

The Revelation Gifts
1. The Word of Wisdom
2. The Word of Knowledge
3. Discerning of Spirits

The Vocal Gifts
1. Prophecy
2. Different Kinds of Tongues
3. Interpretation of Tongues

The Power Gifts
1. Faith
2. Gifts of Healing
3. Working of Miracles

The Revelation Gifts

1. **The Word of Wisdom:** This gift has nothing to do with natural, earthly wisdom. The gift of the word of wisdom is the supernatural revealing of the prophetic future; it is speaking hidden truths of what is not known by way of human wisdom.

   This gift differs from the word of knowledge in that it reveals something about the future. The word of wisdom often operates in conjunction with the gift of prophecy.

   Remember, it is a "word" or a fragment of God's wisdom. God typically does not reveal all of His plan at once, but instead requires us to walk by faith.

   The word of wisdom can manifest in various ways. Joseph interpreted dreams; Daniel received visions,

Ezekiel was caught up in the Spirit. Most commonly, the Holy Spirit speaks into your spirit with a knowing. One may not *understand*, but yet *knows*.

Examples of the word of wisdom:

Jonah:
Jonah 3:4 And Jonah began to enter the city on the first day's walk. Then he cried out and said, "Yet forty days, and Nineveh shall be overthrown!"

Joseph:
Genesis 45:5 But now, do not therefore be grieved or angry with yourselves because you sold me here; for God sent me before you to preserve life. 6 For these two years the famine has been in the land, and there are still five years in which there will be neither plowing nor harvesting. 7 And God sent me before you to preserve a posterity for you in the earth, and to save your lives by a great deliverance.

Paul:
Acts 27:23 For there stood by me this night an angel of the God to whom I belong and whom I serve, 24 saying, "Do not be afraid, Paul; you must be brought before Caesar; and indeed God has granted you all those who sail with you."

Agabus:
Acts 11:28 Then one of them, named Agabus, stood up and showed by the Spirit that there was going to

be a great famine throughout all the world, which also happened in the days of Claudius Caesar.

2. **The Word of Knowledge:** The gift of the word of knowledge is revelation of something that has happened in the past or present that could not be known in the natural.

It may also include a revelation of God's divine will and plan. As with the word of wisdom, it is only a "word" or fragment of God's omniscience.

Jesus was operating in the word of knowledge when He told the Samaritan woman that she'd had five husbands and that the one she was with currently was not her husband (John chapter 4).

Elisha was a man of God that frequently received words of knowledge (2 Kings chapters 5-6). As with the word of wisdom, there are a variety of ways that this gift manifests.

Additional Example of the word of knowledge:

Ananias:
Acts 9:10 Now there was a certain disciple at Damascus named Ananias; and to him the Lord said in a vision, "Ananias." And he said, "Here I am, Lord." 11 So the Lord said to him, "Arise and go to the street called Straight, and inquire at the house of Judas for one called Saul of Tarsus, for behold, he is praying. 12 And in a vision he has seen a man named

Ananias coming in and putting his hand on him, so that he might receive his sight."

3. **Discerning of Spirits:** Discerning of spirits is the supernatural ability given by the Holy Spirit to perceive the source of a spiritual manifestation and determine whether it is of God or from the devil.

   In the end-times, there are many seducing spirits and doctrines of devils and the gift of discerning of spirits is greatly needed in this hour.

   As a word of caution, this is not the gift of suspicion. Additionally, when God gives you discernment, it is not for the purpose of gossip, but rather for prayer. Be Spirit-led in who you share confidential matters with.

   Examples of this gift in the New Testament include Paul in Acts 16 with the woman who had the spirit of divination and Peter in Acts 8 with Simon the sorcerer.

The Vocal Gifts

1. **Prophecy:** People usually think that "prophecy" means to predict (foretell) what will happen in the future. This is frequently confused because people fail to understand that there is a difference between the simple gift of prophecy and the office of a prophet. Prophecy in the New Testament church

carried no prediction with it whatsoever, for "he that prophesies speaks unto men to edification, and exhortation, and comfort" (1 Corinthians 14:3).

- Edification
- Exhortation
- Comfort

Prophecy is divinely inspired and anointed utterance; a supernatural proclamation in a known language. It is the manifestation of the Spirit of God - not of the human intellect.

Prophecy does not come from man's intellect, but from the Spirit of God. As with all nine gifts, it is "as the Spirit wills" (1 Corinthians 12:11) and not as man wills.

Scripture tells us that prophecy within the church should be judged (1 Corinthians 14:29). If it doesn't line up to the Word of God, it should be rejected.

2. **Different Kinds of Tongues:** This gift is the supernatural utterance in an unknown tongue that must be accompanied by an interpretation. When combined with the interpretation, it is the equivalent of prophecy, much in the same way that two nickels equals a dime.

This gift is different from the personal gift of tongues. The personal gift on tongues does not require interpretation, but the public gift of tongues does.

The gifts of tongues and interpretation of tongues is unique from the other seven gifts in that all of the other gifts were functional in the Old Testament and the Gospels. But the gifts of tongues and interpretation of tongues is identified only with the Church age.

When the Spirit wants to manifest this gift through someone, frequently they will begin speaking in tongues under their breath and begin to speak more authoritatively to feel a boldness come upon them; they feel the "need" to speak out. The public gift of tongues carries a unique sound.

There are certain guidelines for this particular gift:

- If there is no interpreter keep silent (1 Corinthians 14:28).
- There should be no more than three messages in tongues in any given worship service (1 Corinthians 14:27)

Note: In a worship service there will be those who are signing or praying in the Spirit, but not in such a way to draw attention or gain an audience. This is acceptable. However, if everyone is silent and one speaks out, there should be an interpretation.

3. **Interpretation of Tongues:** The gift of the interpretation of tongues is the supernatural interpretation of what has been spoken in an unknown tongue. To be clear, this gift is not a *translation* of that tongue, but an interpretation. The tongue may be two minutes in length, but the interpretation only 10 words. However, it has been documented numerous times that a tongue was given in the language known to someone in the crowd, but unknown to the speaker, and the interpretation was completely accurate based on the testimony of the person who spoke the language.

When the Holy Spirit gives someone an interpretation, it may come *during* the tongue or immediately *after*. Sometimes God gives you the entire message before you speak it and other times just a word or two, which must be spoken out in faith before the Spirit gives you more.

The Power Gifts

1. **Faith:** The gift of faith is the supernatural ability to believe God without doubt, overcome unbelief, and visualize what God wants to accomplish.

   This is not individual, ordinary faith. Ordinary faith comes by "hearing and hearing by the word of God" (Rom. 10: 17). The gift of faith will manifest in dire situation where one has "maxed out" their personal faith.

The book of Daniel contains two excellent examples of the gift of faith:

a. Daniel in the lion's den
b. The three Hebrews in the fiery furnace

When Jesus spoke to the fig tree in Matthew 21:19 and cursed it because there was no fruit, this was the gift of faith in operation. The next day, when the disciples passed by, they marveled that it had withered.

2. **Gifts of Healing:** The gift of healings refers to supernatural healing without human aid; it is a special gift to pray for specific diseases. Healing can come through the touch of faith (James 5:14-15); by speaking the word of faith (Luke 7:1-10); or by the presence of God being manifested (Mark 6:56).

This gift is the only one of the nine that is listed in the plural, "gifts" of healing, not gift (singular) of healing. Over the course of church history, there have been numerous examples of men and women who were anointed for healing in specific areas such as vision or cancers. If one person possessed all of the gifts of healing, the temptation for pride would almost surely be too great.

Further, all healing is not physical; supernatural healing can occur for the spiritual, emotional or mental state of a person as well.

All healing under the New Covenant is based on the finished work of Christ on the Cross. By His stripes we were healed (1 Peter 2:24).

3. **Working of Miracles**: A miracle is the supernatural intervention by God in the ordinary course of nature. The miracle often conflicts with the laws of nature. It is the supernatural power of God to intervene and counteract earthly and/or evil forces.

The Bible is filled with miracles. Of course, they are only miracles from man's point of view. To God, they are very ordinary events.

It should be noted that there is a "work or working" involved in this gift and not simply a receiving of miracles. The person being used by God must simply follow the command given by the mother of Jesus at the marriage feast in Cana: "Whatever He says to you, do it" (John 2:5).

Miracles can be healing related or they can be supernatural occurrences outside of the ordinary, such as Peter getting the gold coin from the fish's mouth. When is a healing a miracle? When the healing is instantaneous or of a creative nature.

Keep in mind, nine of the 37 recorded miracles of Jesus were not of a healing nature:

1. Water to wine (John 2:1-11)

2. Catch of fish (Luke 5:1-11)
3. Calms storm (Matthew 8:23-27)
4. Feeds 5,000 (Mark 6:30-44)
5. Walks on water (Matthew 14:22-33)
6. Feeds 4,000 (Mark 8:1-13)
7. Gold coin from fish (Matthew 17:24-27)
8. Withers fig tree (Matthew 21:18-22)
9. Second catch of fish (Matthew 21:4-11

Paul said that all of these gifts or manifestations of the Spirit were as the Spirit wills:

1 Corinthians 12:11 But one and the same Spirit works all these things, distributing to each one individually as He wills.

Points for Reflection

- There are more than nine gifts listed in the New Testament. But there are only nine that are defined as manifestations.

- Diversity and Sameness will flow at the same time when the anointing is present.

- The nine gifts of the Spirit fall into three categories:

  1. Gifts that Reveal something – the Revelation Gifts
  2. Gifts that Say something – the Vocal Gifts
  3. Gifts that Do something – the Power Gifts

- A miracle is the supernatural intervention by God in the ordinary course of nature.

Counterfeit Anointing

There is, what I will call, a counterfeit anointing. Wherever there is a genuine article, there will also be a counterfeit. It must be remembered that Lucifer was the "anointed cherub" before he fell from heaven.

> **Ezekiel 28:14-15**
> **14 "You were the anointed cherub who covers; I established you; you were on the holy mountain of God; you walked back and forth in the midst of fiery stones.**
> **15 You were perfect in your ways from the day you were created, till iniquity was found in you.**

Given his background, it's no wonder that Satan knows how to counterfeit the anointing. The Bible further reveals that Satan and his messengers can and do appear as "angels of light" (2 Corinthians 11:14). God's servants must operate in the discernment of the Holy Spirit.

Webster's defines "counterfeit" as, "made in imitation of something else with intent to deceive." Satan is a master deceiver. He intends to dupe folks with his imitation. As an example, the founder of a cult wrote, "We believe in the gift of tongues, prophecy, revelation, visions, healing, interpretation of tongues, and so forth." Since this religion does not have the true Holy Spirit, any manifestation of said gifts would be counterfeit.

More common to the Christian faith, especially in charismatic circles, are those who exploit God's people for material gain. I attended a pastor's conference back in the early 90's. The host was a well-known young pastor whose ministry had exploded in growth. In the night service, with several thousand in attendance, a minister on the platform gave a prophecy that there were several pastors there who were supposed to give $1,500 and if they obeyed, God would bless their churches.

This word brought a stir to the congregation. Shortly thereafter, the host pastor got up and started speaking. He echoed his approval for the word given, but then said something that startled and alarmed me. The pastor said, "Let's just make it an even thousand." I'm not sure how that hits you, but for me, it set off the red flag warning in my spirit that the manifestations and anointing of the Holy Spirit were being misused and manipulated for material gain.

If the Holy Spirit truly said to give $1,500 (which I was skeptical of to begin with), how can man then override Him to change His word to $1,000? Yet, sadly, many preachers came running forward with their thousand-dollar-checks. If preachers can be easily duped, where does that leave us in the discernment department?

In this same conference, I was instructed how to lie my way out of a preaching engagement if a better offer came along afterwards. I never again participated in that man's ministry, even though he had a dynamic preaching ability.

1 Peter 5:2-3

2 Shepherd the flock of God which is among you, serving as overseers, not by compulsion but willingly, not for dishonest gain but eagerly;

3 nor as being lords over those entrusted to you, but being examples to the flock

People will manipulate and imitate the anointing for the purpose of dishonest gain. Look for shepherds who make themselves an example to the flock, not ones who have an entourage and an unapproachable persona. Jesus said that the greatest among you would be your servant (Matthew 23:11).

Balaam

The story of Balaam in the Old Testament is an interesting case. Balaam, basically, was a pagan diviner-for-hire. God spoke through him, but He also spoke through Balaam's donkey. Neither were fit leaders to follow.

> **Numbers 24:2 And Balaam raised his eyes, and saw Israel encamped according to their tribes; and the Spirit of God came upon him.**

This verse shows us that the anointing – the Spirit of God – came upon him. Yet in the book of Revelation, we read that Jesus chastised the church at Pergamos for holding the "doctrine of Balaam."

> **Revelation 2:14 But I have a few things against you, because you have there those who hold the doctrine of Balaam, who taught Balak to put a stumbling block**

before the children of Israel, to eat things sacrificed to idols, and to commit sexual immorality.

So, we see a man who was a diviner to be hired out for the god of your choice, being anointed by the Spirit of God to deliver a message. We also know that he was used to put a stumbling block before the children of Israel. When examining one's ministry and anointing, there are more to be looked at than gifting and inspiration.

Spirit of divination

In Acts chapter 16, Paul and his company came to Philippi. They were there under the direct revelation of the Holy Spirit (v 9-10). Everything was going good. Prayer meetings were being held at the riverside, just outside the city. In fact, a woman named Lydia became the first Christian convert in Europe in those meetings (v 14-15). All of the Holy Ghost activity began to draw attention, and Satan was on the alert. The devil always wants to disrupt the start of a revival before it has a chance to get going. A girl who was possessed with the spirit of divination entered the picture.

> **Acts 16:16-18**
> **16 Now it happened, as we went to prayer, that a certain slave girl possessed with a spirit of divination met us, who brought her masters much profit by fortune-telling.**
> **17 This girl followed Paul and us, and cried out, saying, "These men are the servants of the Most High God, who proclaim to us the way of salvation."**
> **18 And this she did for many days.**

But Paul, greatly annoyed, turned and said to the spirit, "I command you in the name of Jesus Christ to come out of her." And he came out that very hour.

Please notice that the girl who was possessed was saying the right words: "These men are the servants of the Most High God, who proclaim to us the way of salvation." When the counterfeit anointing is in operation, it is not always identified by the words. Satan is a master deceiver. As believers, we need the discernment that comes from the Holy Spirit. In this case, Paul listened to this for several days and became agitated in the spirit. The King James uses the word *grieved*, which I think is an accurate translation. When the counterfeit is in operation, there is a grieving in the spirit of Spirit-led believers. Sometimes it takes a little while to put your finger on it, but eventually we figure it out.

The Greek word translated "divination" in verse 16 *pythona*, which literally means "python" – the serpent. A python seizes its prey in its coils and kills it by constriction. This is also true spiritually; the spirit of divination or python slowly squeezes the life of God out of the environment until there is nothing but spiritual death. This has happened to numerous churches and ministries that have allowed this demonic spirit to gain a stronghold.

Paul cast the spirit out! He set the girl free in the power of the name of Jesus Christ. She was delivered from that hour. When I was sitting under the ministry of Lester Sumrall, I saw this same scenario played out many times. People from all over the world would come each Sunday to be delivered and Brother Sumrall would command the demons to come out in Jesus' name and they obeyed. There were no shenanigans, just power through His name and obedience by the demons.

Not only was the girl set free but the spirit of python that possessed her was also controlling the region. It broke open the heavens in Philippi. There was not immediate revival. Instead, Paul and Silas got thrown into jail because her masters realized that their source of income was over. You know the rest of the story. Paul and Silas praised God anyway and God sent an earthquake to loose them from prison and brought revival to the city. But it all started by bringing down the stronghold of divination.

As previously mentioned, during the healing revivals of the 1950's, men and women, who were often genuinely gifted, got out of the anointing and operated with familiar spirits and the spirit of divination. How could this be? The Holy Spirit does not come under the control of any man. He cannot, and will not be turned off and on like a water faucet to suit man's agenda. In the long run, many of these men and women ended their lives caught up in error and heresy.

Remember, Jesus said that there would be counterfeits and false prophets who performed lying signs and wonders.

> **Matthew 7:22-23**
> **22 Many will say to me in that day, Lord, Lord, have we not prophesied in thy name? and in thy name have cast out devils? and in thy name done many wonderful works?**
> **23 And then will I profess unto them, I never knew you: depart from me, ye that work iniquity.**

We are instructed to know them by their fruit (Matthew 7:20). Gifting, charisma, personality can all go into making someone believable, but of what does their fruit testify? Appearances alone can cause one to mistakenly follow a counterfeit. Even Satan himself can transform into an angel of light (2 Corinthians 11:14).

Make everything line up to the Word of God. Listen to the Holy Spirit and guard your heart from deception.

Points for Reflection

- Wherever there is a genuine article, there will also be a counterfeit.

- People will manipulate and imitate the anointing for the purpose of dishonest gain.

- When examining one's ministry and anointing, there are more to be looked at than gifting and inspiration.

- The spirit of divination or python slowly squeezes the life of God out of the environment until there is nothing but spiritual death.

Sensual Not Having The Spirit

Jude 19 These are sensual persons, who cause divisions, not having the Spirit.

Jude draws a distinction in this verse and refers to those who are sensual as "not having the Spirit." What does it mean to be sensual? The original Greek word is *psychikos* and means, "to be controlled by the appetites and passions." What James is saying is that a believer cannot be controlled by his appetites and passions and still be controlled by the Spirit. The former will cancel the latter.

As Christians, we must guard our hearts from the "little foxes that spoil the vine" (Song of Songs 2:15). If we are not careful, little things will begin to take the place of fellowship with Christ. Hebrews 12:1 makes it clear that it is not only sin that hinders us but "things" as well – the things that weigh us down.

Appetite speaks to more areas than food. Although, food has become a major problem for so many people. It has always struck me as peculiar when a severely overweight man preaches on the power of fasting. Gaining control of the appetite in the area of food is more than a one or two week exercise. To fast for a week and then go back to over indulgence is counter-productive if not hypocritical. But let's apply that same principle to other areas. If we aren't careful, we will allow things such as television, sports, hobbies, etc. become idols in our lives. Anything that takes priority over God in our hearts becomes an idol.

If I am not careful, I can allow my love for sports to take too large of a place in my attention. At one point in my life, when I wasn't walking closely with God, I would watch every football game that came across the airwaves. I would record games on the VCR (this was in the days prior to DVRs) that were on at the same time or when I wasn't home. To make matter worse, if my favorite team lost, it would put me in a bad mood for a day or two. It became an idol in my life that had to be destroyed.

Social media in today's world has become an insatiable appetite for many. They can never get enough. They must check for updates constantly to see who may have commented on their status. It becomes a major distraction from the important areas of our lives – things such as our relationship with God and family. There is nothing wrong with Facebook, Twitter or any other form of social media as long as they are used in moderation. In fact, they can be great tools to advance the gospel. But we must guard our hearts at all times from allowing it to cross the line and becoming a compulsion.

In fact, the Internet has completely opened up a new dimension for both good and evil that has never existed in the history or mankind. While there is much good that can come from the web, such as learning resources, there are many traps of Satan for the man and woman of God when they go online. This is a hidden area that can strip the anointing of God off someone's life, even if no one sees the activity that leads to destruction.

The admonition to guard one's heart becomes all the more important when getting online.

Guarding Your Heart While Online

The Word of God tells us to "guard your heart with all diligence." In real life there are very distinct signals to watch for when it comes to protecting our hearts. We all have what we call our "personal space." We immediately get uncomfortable upon invasion. However, when online there is a greater tendency to let our guards down. After all, we can just click the X button if we think it's gone too far, right? If it were only that easy. Just *one* picture... just *one* flirtatious text... Below, I have listed five areas to guard your heart while online. You may think that none of them apply to you, but my inclination is that each and every one of us is subject to these forces every time we go online. The time to guard your heart is prior to entry of one of them. After one or more has gained entrance, a different teaching is needed – one of deliverance.

1. Pornography: What else could come at the top of this list? As we already discussed, pornography is prevalent within the church, and unfortunately, many of its leaders have also fallen prey. Pornography will destroy your spiritual life and your marriage. My mentor, Lester Sumrall, used to say that "sin will take you further than you wanted to go, keep you longer than you wanted to stay, and cost you more than you were willing to pay." These words of admonishment are no truer than as it relates to pornography. Pornography is very addictive. The addictive aspect of pornography has a biological substrate, with dopamine hormone release acting as one of the mechanisms for forming the transmission pathway to pleasure centers of the brain.

In the Family Research Counsel's report on pornography it is noted that men are six times more likely to view pornography than women. However, the study also identified that women were more inclined to engage in chat of a sexual nature. Jesus said that if your right eye causes you to sin then pluck it out (Matthew 5:29). In other words, get rid of whatever is causing you to sin. If you can't get on the Internet without being tempted to view pornography then stop going on the Internet.

2. Emotional Affairs: This is where the enemy is subtle in his attack. A married person starts finding emotional fulfillment through online relationships with the opposite sex. It may seem harmless at first; after all, it's just talk or chat, right? That may be where it starts, but it too often ends with wrecked lives. Consider these remarks from the Relationship Institute:

Is your marriage actually in danger the moment you start investing time in a relationship with anyone who isn't your husband or wife? Yes, according to the Relationship Institute, which says that an emotional connection is much more dangerous than a physical one. "Some argue that an emotional affair is harmless," says a spokesman, "because it is more of a casual relationship than traditional cheating. However, the intimate nature of the communication, in addition to the emotional investment made by the people involved, places an emotional affair on the same level — or worse — as traditional cheating."

There are a million ways to justify it, but if it were pure there would be no need to rationalize the need. There's nothing wrong with interacting with the opposite sex online, in a wholesome manner. But when it starts extending to frequent emails and text messages, sharing innermost thoughts and feelings, it is sin. You are taking something away from your spouse, intimacy, and giving it to another man or woman. You may say, "It's just friendship," and that may be the case for you, but perhaps not so for the other person whom you are leading along. If you find yourself going down this trail, put a stop to it. Jesus clearly told us in Matthew 5:28 that adultery was a matter of the heart, not just the body. Intimacy with the opposite sex, physical and/or emotional, is to be limited to the marriage relationship.

3. Foolish Talking: It is easy to create a different persona online than you are in real life. After all, you can be a tough guy, even if you do weigh 132 pounds, or a Casanova, even if you don't have any front teeth. A little role-play may not be terrible. However, when a Christian begins to carry on like the world with filthy talking, hiding behind an anonymous user name, it is sin and it is displeasing to the Lord. Ephesians 5:3-4 says, "But fornication and all uncleanness or covetousness, let it not even be named among you, as is fitting for saints; neither filthiness, nor foolish talking, nor coarse jesting, which are not fitting, but rather giving of thanks."

Guard your heart against departmentalizing your life. In other words, having one personality at work, another at home, another online, another at church, etc. The Word of God tells us that we are ambassadors of Christ (2 Corinthians 5:20). That means we are called to represent Him at all times.

4. Addiction: The Internet can be a valuable tool as well as a source of entertainment, neither of which are wrong. However, when a Christian spends inordinate amounts of time online, escaping from family, friends and real world activities then the Internet has become an idol that needs to be torn down. The same is true if one is consumed with watching television or reading romance novels endlessly. Scripture teaches us that all things should be done in moderation. Do you feel like you are missing something if you can't get online? This is a warning sign.

Romans chapter 6 tells us that whatever we yield ourselves to, we become its slave to obey. Instead, we should be slaves to God. Is there anything in your life that you could not walk away from if the Lord put His finger on it? If so, it is an idol, an addiction. Ephesians 5:16 tells us to "Redeem the time, because the days are evil." Ultimately, where we invest the majority of our free time is what is most important to us, by default. If you don't think so, just ask those around you.

5. Being a Stumbling Block: I Corinthians 8:9 tells us that it's not all about ourselves. Imagine that! *But beware lest somehow this liberty of yours become a stumbling block to those who are weak.* God holds us accountable for our brothers and sisters. Paul also wrote in Romans 14:13, "not to put a stumbling block or a cause to fall in our brother's way."

How can we be a stumbling block online? There are several ways. One way is to provoke another to anger intentionally. After a while, we learn the hot buttons of those in our online communities and it is easy to set them off. I have been guilty of this and I have asked God to help me in this area.

Another way is to engage in what some would consider "harmless" flirting, with sexual innuendo. We talked about this in point number 3.

Of course, the most thought of way of being a stumbling block is with pictures. And as noted in point number 1, men are six times more likely to stumble in this area than women. Pictures should not be posted online that are of a sensual or seductive nature. I Timothy 2:9 says, "That the women adorn themselves in modest apparel, with propriety and moderation." The same holds true for men. Our need for attention should not be the cause of stumbling for someone else.

As Christians, before we take any action, we should ask ourselves, "How does this affect those around me?" This is a central message of the gospel. To think that our liberty allows us to do as we choose is a deceptive lie.

I am thankful for the Internet. It allows me to communicate teachings from the Word of God, to get to know people from all over the world. But I need to guard my heart because Satan walks about as a roaring lion seeking those whom he may devour (I Peter 5:8).

Lust
A big problem in the church world today is the issue of pornography. Since the advent of the internet, it has become easy to anonymously pollute yourself with the filth of pornography via the web. Surveys have shown that anywhere from 33% to 50% of pastors have viewed pornography in the past 12 months. Further, the same is true for 70% of all Christian men from the age of 18 to 34.

Satan knows that the fastest way to take a man of God down is through the lust of the flesh. The book of Proverbs gives many warnings about this, including the following verse:

Proverbs 7:26 For she hath cast down many wounded: yea, many strong men have been slain by her.

When a man of God is spiritually weak or wounded, Satan wants to pounce on him with the temptations of lust. Please pray for your spiritual leaders and pastors. They are human with weaknesses, as all others. It is only through the power of the Holy Spirit that any of us can live this victorious life in Christ.

Keeping our Passion for God
God wants us to have a passion for Him. David prayed, "As the deer pants for the water brooks, so pants my soul for You, O God" (Psalm 42:1). When our passion turns to other things, the anointing of God upon our lives decreases.

The Steward of God

Titus 1:7 For a bishop must be blameless, as a steward of God, not self-willed...

I discovered something very fascinating about this verse a while back. We all know what self-willed means, but I think that this word is a very poor translation. The original Greek word is *authadés* and is a compound word. The prefix simply means, "self," as translated. But the second word does not mean "willed." It is the Greek word *hēdomai* and means "pleasing." So, a better translation would be *self-pleasing*. But it isn't just any kind of self-pleasing; it is self-pleasing of a sensual nature. The English word *hedonism* is derived from this word *hēdomai*. Hedonism is the pursuit of sensual self-indulgence.

The bishop of God – the leader of God's flock, cannot be given to self-indulgence. It has brought many men of God down. The heart must be guarded at all costs.

Points for Reflection

The original Greek word is *psychikos* and means, "to be controlled by the appetites and passions."

As Christians, we must guard our hearts from the "little foxes that spoil the vine" (Song of Songs 2:15).

The Internet has completely opened up a new dimension for both good and evil that has never existed in the history or mankind.

Sin will take you further than you wanted to go, keep you longer than you wanted to stay, and cost you more than you were willing to pay.

As Christians, before we take any action, we should ask ourselves, "How does this affect those around me?"

God's leaders must not be given to self-gratification, especially of a sensual nature.

Understanding Your Anointing

There are general anointings that will come upon all believers as they do the Lord's work, and then there are specific anointings that are unique to one's calling. For example, every preacher is not called to be a teacher and consequently, will not have the anointing to teach. That doesn't mean that he can't teach at all, as the Bible tells us that all elders should be "apt to teach" (2 Timothy 2:24). But there is a difference between being *apt* to teach and having a teaching anointing.

One prominent minister was a teacher, by gift, but he didn't always have the gift of teaching; subsequently, he didn't have the anointing to teach. He pastored for almost 10 years and had spent a total of about 12 years in full-time ministry when the Lord gave him the gift and anointing to teach. Up until that point, he says that he absolutely hated teaching.

One day, after 12 years, the Lord told him, "You are ready to enter the first phase of your ministry." This was quite stunning to this minister. But teaching was his true gift and anointing; he had just not entered into it yet. Whenever he had to teach, he dreaded it and couldn't wait for it to be over. After he received the gift and experienced the anointing to teach, it was completely different.

How he described receiving the gift was interesting, may be of some use to others. He said that he was walking through his parsonage one day, when he felt something drop down inside of him. It was the gift of teaching. He said that it clicked down inside of him like a coin drops inside of a pay phone. I realize that some readers don't know what I'm talking about at this point. Nonetheless, the year was 1943 and from that time until he died in 2003, this man functioned as a teacher in the body of Christ.

Now, everyone may not experience this type of singular moment when they *know that they know* their particular anointing. For me, God inscribed it indelibly on my heart, over time, as I sought Him. Since that period, I have had those singular moments when God spoke, but the foundation of my calling goes back to those original days, months and years of seeking.

I often get asked, "How do I know what my anointing is?" Generally, I quote a couple of scriptures, tell them that it takes a little time and experience, and then, lastly, I point out that it's important to go where the needs are and try to help. That last part is usually the missing ingredient for people. We want to stay in our rooms with the door closed and figure out what our anointing is. The best way to begin to learn is to get out of your comfort zones... stretch out and minister to someone who is hurting. Experience the different ways that God uses you. Grow from the experiences and keep studying the Word and seeking God. As you grow, you will become more in tune with the Holy Spirit.

These experiences of stepping out will add a depth to your anointing that will be marked. Character is developed during these experiences. When gifting and character merge, the anointing of God is the strongest.

**When gifting and character merge, the
anointing of God is the strongest**

My favorite author when I was first saved was Watchman Nee (he still is, for that matter). Watchman was used greatly by God in China during the first part of the twentieth century. In fact, he spent the last 20 years of his life in a Chinese prison for the cause of Christ. One day, one of Watchman's students asked him, "Teacher, how long does it take to prepare a sermon?" Watchman responded, "About 20 years." I'm not sure if the student grasped what he was saying, but it resonated with me. With gifting from God, one can study and prepare and be used by God, but real depth in the anointing comes through experience and time.

The key is to keep applying yourself in the areas that God has called you. Early in my ministry, I wanted to start a church in a particular area. However, nothing was working out. It seemed that all of the doors were closed. I did not want to see it. I persisted. Finally, one night I got quiet before the Lord and asked Him what was happening. God spoke to me in a clear and direct manner: "You have many things to suffer and endure, but I will tell you when the time is right." I did not want to hear this but I could not deny His voice. Later, I understood why I needed to wait on this particular endeavor. God's will is always perfect and His timing is always right.

Since that day, I have learned many things of eternal value, about the anointing of God. The Lord has designed this to be a process that is developed through our daily walk. Spiritual understanding is critical to accomplishing God's will in our lives.

Abide in Your Calling

The Word of God instructs us to "abide in our calling" (1 Corinthians 7:20). This means to stay with the anointing that God has given you and don't try to copy what another is doing.

There is a passage of Scripture in Paul's second letter to the Corinthians, chapter 10, which is rarely discussed. In this passage, Paul specifically tells us that each person has a measure, limit, or sphere to his or her ministry. In other words, there is a scope to how big your work in the Lord will be. It can be frustrating if you feel that your measure is too small. The tendency is to measure ourselves by comparison with others, which is unwise. We are to evaluate the work we do for the Lord based solely on obedience to His call and the sphere He's called us to.

> **2 Corinthians 10:12-16**
> **12 For we dare not class ourselves or compare ourselves with those who commend themselves. But they, measuring themselves by themselves, and comparing themselves among themselves, are not wise.**
> **13 We, however, will not boast beyond measure, but within the limits of the sphere which God appointed us—a sphere which especially includes you.**
> **14 For we are not overextending ourselves (as though *our authority* did not extend to you), for it was to you that we came with the gospel of Christ;**

15 not boasting of things beyond measure, *that is,* in other men's labors, but having hope, *that* as your faith is increased, we shall be greatly enlarged by you in our sphere,

16 to preach the gospel in the *regions* beyond you, *and* not to boast in another man's sphere of accomplishment.

The encouraging part about this passage is that in verse 15, Paul says that our sphere can be enlarged. Be faithful. Abide in your anointing. Don't compare with big ministries and mega churches, allowing the devil to minimize your impact. If you are faithful over the small, God will make you ruler over much (Matthew 25:23). What is "much?" Much isn't what someone else has, but the fullness of God's plan and sphere for your ministry.

God's Calling vs. Man's

Lastly, there are lots of religious people who will try to disqualify you from being used by God. They have the spirit of a Pharisee, with their list of rules. The good news is that if God called you, there is nothing that man can do to take away from your calling. Conversely, if God hasn't called you, there is nothing that man can add to make up for the absence of His call. In other words, the only ordination that truly matters is the one that comes from God. Man may confirm what God has done; however, a piece of paper will not produce the anointing.

I have heard some make the excuse that they are called to preach, but their church or their pastor "won't let them preach." Consequently, they do nothing with their calling. They simply bemoan their lack of opportunity. Friend, if God has called you

109

to preach, you will find opportunities to herald the gospel. When God called me, I preached on the street corners every day for two years. I preached in homeless shelters and nursing homes. Listen to what the apostle Paul said regarding his call to preach:

> **1 Corinthians 9:16 For if I preach the gospel, I have nothing to boast of, for necessity is laid upon me; yes, woe is me if I do not preach the gospel!**

If you have the woe, then you have to go! There are no excuses that will stand up at the Judgment Seat of Christ.

Points for Reflection

There are general anointings that will come upon all believers as they do the Lord's work, and then there are specific anointings that are unique to one's calling.

The best way to begin to learn where your anointing lies is to get out of your comfort zone and minister to someone who is hurting.

When gifting and character merge, the anointing of God is the strongest.

We are to evaluate the work we do for the Lord based solely on obedience to His call and the sphere He's called us to.

Factors that Affect the Anointing

There are numerous variables that that have the potential to affect the anointing of the Holy Spirit – either positively or negatively. In this final chapter, we will look at some of these different factors. We will begin with the negative ones.

Negative Influences on the Anointing

Unbelief: Jesus could do no mighty work in His hometown because of their unbelief (Mark 6:1-6). Sometimes, we think we are operating in faith, but the reality is that we are not. Keep in mind that Jesus once told a man who had just walked on water that he only had a "little faith." If that's a little, what's a lot? And more to the point, what is none?

Tradition: Jesus said that the tradition of men would render the Word of God ineffective (Mark 7:13). It's easy to look outside of our circle and identify the traditions of men in other groups and denominations. It is much harder to identify them in your own life and group. For some reason, we think that God will honor our traditions, even if they are extra-Biblical.

Falling down or being "slain in the Spirit" became a Charismatic tradition within the past 30-40 years. Why do I say that? Because there are really no examples in Scripture. The ones used are taken out of context. Am I saying that the experience is fake? Not necessarily. But it has gotten to the point in some circles that people believe that you can't be healed unless you fall down. If that were the case, then no one was healed under the ministry of Jesus. God can heal people standing up, sitting down or lying down. We should not take an experience and form a doctrine with it.

Judgmental Attitudes

Let me provide an example of a judgmental attitude that quenches the anointing. I live in Arizona and in the summer it gets very hot. I believe in modesty, but there are times that people, especially young people and kids, will wear something to church that wouldn't be described as modest. It has been repeated to me that someone said, "If so-and-so wears something like that to church again, I'm getting up and walking out." That is a Pharisee spirit. Now keep in mind that we are talking about the length of shorts and such, not exposing one's self.

Correcting someone's attire takes five minutes, but I'm not sure how long it takes to correct an attitude such as that. Some folks think that means they are "holy." I believe, that such attitudes quench the Holy Spirit. Now, that's no license to dress immodestly, but when we start threatening to walk out of the church because everyone doesn't meet our standards, we have clogged up the flow of the Holy Spirit's ability to move. God meets people on whatever level they are on, not just on the level that we personally set.

The same is true for those with tattoos or piercings. These outward things do not prevent the Holy Spirit from moving and changing lives, but the judgmental attitudes of some will remove the anointing.

> **Matthew 7:3-5**
> **3 And why do you look at the speck in your brother's eye, but do not consider the plank in your own eye?**
> **4 Or how can you say to your brother, 'Let me remove the speck from your eye'; and look, a plank is in your own eye?**
> **5 Hypocrite! First remove the plank from your own eye, and then you will see clearly to remove the speck from your brother's eye.**

Distractions

Sometimes, when I'm preaching, someone will yell out, "Tell us more about that! But that might me all that the Holy Spirit directs me to say on that matter, at that time. I might need to respond back, "Would you prefer that I listen to you, or the Holy Spirit?" Usually, though, I just ignore it and move on. But, that's what I am thinking sometimes.

I also have people trying to wave me down, occasionally, while I am preaching. I realize that they are simply trying to get my attention, but I have told people that unless the building is on fire, to refrain from waving their arms. This is a distraction and can break the flow of the anointing.

Further, when praying for people, the music can be too loud and hinder the ability to hear from the Spirit. The same is true when there are too many people moving about, around the person receiving ministry.

These seem like small matters, but they can be major distractions when the Holy Spirit is moving. There will always be a minimal amount of distraction and activity; we cannot control everything that occurs. But when the Holy Spirit is moving, we should be careful not to disrupt the flow of the anointing.

In my church, during personal ministry time, I allow people to leave the sanctuary if they need to leave. However, I ask them to be quiet and respectful. I allow this for two reasons: 1) Respect is a two-way street and I respect other people's schedules and commitments; and 2) I need the room to be plugged in and engaged with the Spirit. If people are standing around wishing it were over so they can leave, this will quench the Spirit. We live in a busy world and there's no need to have people remain unless they want to be there.

Poor Time Management
I am constantly amazed at how God's people misuse time and then blame the Holy Spirit, as if He's the one making them ramble on. When the church comes together in one place, it is for the purpose of edification. Everything that is done should have a razor sharp focus. Too often, churches start 5-10 minutes late, proceed without direction or inspiration, ramble on with announcements, turn 2-minute testimonies into 10-minute ones, sing song after song just because they're on the song list, and give sermons that end up chasing rabbit trails. They then cap it off by saying, "We just let the Lord have His way…"

There is nothing wrong with having a time schedule and operating within it. That is not to say that you shouldn't go past, if the Holy Spirit is directing. But when there is a schedule, there is more focus. When I first started preaching, I went entirely too long. I felt like if I had more written on my sermon outline that I needed to give it all. Unfortunately, when we go too long, we sometimes undo the good that has been accomplished.

The church needs to be the church 24/7, but when we meet on Sundays, we have a limited amount of time, whether that be 90 minutes, two hours, or however long. It is important to come in prayed up and ready to go. The entire focus should be on glorifying Jesus and on the edification of the body.

> **1 Corinthians 14:26 How is it then, brethren? Whenever you come together, each of you has a psalm, has a teaching, has a tongue, has a revelation, has an interpretation. Let all things be done for edification.**

Performance

There is a recent trend within the church to become more performance oriented. This is apparent with the music area, but is found also in the preaching. A worship team's assignment is to worship God, not to perform songs. The problem is that you can't just assemble the best musicians and singers and have a worship team. The team must be comprised of worshippers who are also skilled musicians and singers.

As noted, the performance problem is also found in the pulpit. Preachers feel the need to be entertainers, with jokes and stories. Being a preacher of the Word is not about becoming a personality. When the emphasis gets placed on these fleshly attributes, the anointing is nowhere to be found. Sadly, many people would rather be entertained than have an encounter with God.

Disengagement

To start with, it is usually difficult to get people to engage – to fully participate. Anointed worship will draw people into God's presence. Then, there are transitional moments within the church gathering (e.g., announcements). The challenge is to keep people engaged in the Spirit. Sometimes, when I get up to preach, I feel that the momentum has shifted or even ceased. I will push against it in the spirit and the Holy Spirit will anoint the Word being preached.

Most importantly, near the end of the meeting, when God wants to confirm His Word with signs following, it is a challenge to keep people from disengaging and mentally preparing to leave. The first thing that I do when I stop preaching to exhort the people to stay with me in the Spirit. This is the most important part of the meeting. We cannot afford to checkout before God is through. Please remember the importance of this when you are at church. I realize you may be hungry or have a scheduled appointment, but God can do more in five minutes than we can in a lifetime. The yoke of oppression is destroyed because of the anointing.

People Pleasing

"People pleasing" is a trap that is easy to fall into. "So and so doesn't like it when I preach on "such and such," so I will avoid it today. When we run the Holy Spirit's promptings through the *people-pleasing filter*, we quench the anointing. Some people are always looking to be offended. If those being used by the Lord in a given situation, focus on not offending people, they will miss what the Spirit wants to say and do.

Listen to the words of the apostle Paul:

Galatians 1:10 (NLT) Obviously, I'm not trying to win the approval of people, but of God. If pleasing people were my goal, I would not be Christ's servant.

The Sin of Familiarity

The sin of familiarity occurs when a person diminishes the gifting on someone's life just because they know him or her on a personal level. Perhaps the known flaws or shortcomings of the person cause the recipient to doubt that God could use him or her. Even when that is not the case, there is still a tendency to diminish someone who is known versus someone who is unknown. This was even the case with the ministry of Jesus in His hometown. They saw Jesus grow up and knew Him on a personal level. His family still lived there. They couldn't get past the natural association enough to receive from the Spirit.

The Bible says that Jesus could do no mighty work there, because of their lack of honor.

Mark 6:3-5

3 Is this not the carpenter, the Son of Mary, and brother of James, Joses, Judas, and Simon? And are not His sisters here with us?" So they were offended at Him.

4 But Jesus said to them, "A prophet is not without honor except in his own country, among his own relatives, and in his own house."

5 Now He could do no mighty work there, except that He laid His hands on a few sick people and healed *them.*

Positive Influences on the Anointing

Basically, we could say that all of the opposites of the negative factors are the positive ones. But let's discuss some specifics.

Faith in God

The Word says that "without faith it is impossible to please God" (Hebrews 11:6). When we do the works of the ministry, if we do not believe that God will respond then we are defeated before we start. Too often, we allow failed attempts from the past to hinder our faith. I have often said that if I pray for 100 people to be healed and none of them are, it does not weaken God's promise one bit. Conversely, if all 100 are healed, it does not strengthen God's promise. We must let the naked Word of God stand on it's own. If you want to operate in the anointing of the Holy Spirit, keep believing! Don't allow what you see with your eyes to stop the force of faith in your ministry.

2 Corinthians 5:7 For we walk by faith, not by sight.

Compassion

There are some gifted ministers in the body of Christ, but sometimes, compassion seems to be at an all-time low. This is because compassion must be birthed through experience. There must be a mile, somewhere along the way, that you have walked in someone's shoes.

I had a medical procedure done a while back. There were postoperative complications. It was a very hard time in my life. I could not understand why God wasn't healing me. After several weeks, God healed me. I woke up one morning and the problem

119

was gone. But in the process, I learned more about compassion for the sick than I had in over 20 years of ministry. We don't get to choose the tools that God uses to teach us the lessons that we need to learn.

Jesus always operated out of compassion for people.

> **Matthew 14:14 And when Jesus went out He saw a great multitude; and He was moved with compassion for them, and healed their sick.**

> **Matthew 15:32 Now Jesus called His disciples to *Himself* and said, "I have compassion on the multitude...**

> **Matthew 20:34 So Jesus had compassion and touched their eyes. And immediately their eyes received sight, and they followed Him.**

> **Mark 6:34 And Jesus, when He came out, saw a great multitude and was moved with compassion for them, because they were like sheep not having a shepherd. So He began to teach them many things.**

Jesus is always our model of ministry. We must allow God to develop compassion in us for the lost and hurting. Also, notice that Jesus never compared the person He was ministering to with the last person He healed. He didn't say, "You think you have it bad, you should've seen the last guy... he couldn't even walk!" There is no problem too big or too small for Jesus to involve Himself with. When ministering to people, care about them with God's compassion.

Prayer Warriors

Satan will always oppose the anointing. He knows that when the anointing of the Holy Spirit is present, chains of darkness are broken. Specific to a church meeting, when there is resistance in the spirit, it is important that there are prayer warriors who recognize this and will pray.

Listen to the words of the Apostle Paul, as he requested prayer for his ministry:

> **Ephesians 6:18-19**
> **18 praying always with all prayer and supplication in the Spirit, being watchful to this end with all perseverance and supplication for all the saints—**
> **19 and for me, that utterance may be given to me, that I may open my mouth boldly to make known the mystery of the gospel.**

It's no coincidence that Paul wrote this as the concluding remarks about the armor of God. Anointed utterance is surely the spoils of spiritual warfare. Satan does not want the anointed Word of God going forth. Jesus said that when man knows the truth that the truth would make him free (John 8:32).

There are times when I am preaching and begin to feel resistance in the spirit. The utterance from the Holy Spirit is being fought against. Having a group of prayer warriors in the congregation who will combat this will defeat the enemy. The Word of God is not bound (2 Timothy 2:9)!

Waiting

Waiting can be difficult, especially for the flesh. As believers we must be conditioned to wait upon the Lord in our personal lives. God works on His schedule, not ours. As servants of the Lord in public ministry, we must also learn to wait upon the Holy Spirit.

Romans 12:7 (KJV) Let us wait on our ministering.

Too often we rush ahead with our programs and leave the Holy Spirit out of the proceedings. To operate in the anointing, waiting is essential. There are times when I know that the Holy Spirit isn't through, but I don't know *what* He wants to do. So I wait. He is always faithful to reveal His plans as long as we remain in a surrender mode. Sometimes, the greatest miracles occur during these times of waiting upon the Lord.

The key is to get the others in the room to wait also. People tend to get antsy and restless, physically and mentally. I always exhort people to stay connected and engaged during the waiting period. Waiting should be done with expectancy that God is working.

Points for Reflection

- Jesus could do no mighty work in His hometown because of their unbelief.

- Jesus said that the tradition of men would render the Word of God ineffective.

- Outward things such as tattoos do not prevent the Holy Spirit from moving and changing lives, but the judgmental attitudes of some will remove the anointing.

- When the Holy Spirit is moving, we should be careful not to disrupt the flow of the anointing.

- God's people often misuse time and then blame the Holy Spirit when it is simply poor time management.

- When God's people stay spiritually and mentally engaged and united in faith, great things will occur.

- Jesus always operated out of compassion for people.

- Sometimes, the greatest miracles occur during these times of waiting upon the Lord.

Other Books by David Chapman

Blood Covenant

The Believer's Deliverance Handbook

The Fullness of the Spirit

Modern Day Apostles

The Pattern and the Glory

Thus Saith The Lord

The Power of Praise: 7 Hebrew Words for Praise

Knowing God's Will & Walking In His Blessing

Made in the USA
Monee, IL
25 August 2020